WANTING TO FOLLOW, FORCED TO LEAD

Elizabeth

Baker

Tyndale House
Publishers, Inc.
Wheaton, Illinois

Library of Congress Cataloging-in-Publication Data

Baker, Elizabeth, date
    Wanting to Follow, forced to lead / Elizabeth Baker.
        p.   cm.
    ISBN 0-8423-8279-8
    1. Marriage—Religious aspects—Christianity.   2. Wives—Religious
life.   3.Husbands—Religious life.   4.Parenting—Religious
aspects—Christianity.   I. Title.
BV835.B315   1991
248.8'435—dc20   91-23226

Scripture quotations, unless otherwise noted, are taken from the *Holy Bible,* King James Version. Scripture quotations marked NIV are taken from the *Holy Bible,* New International Version. Copyright © 1973, 1978, 1984 International Bible Society. Used by permission of Zondervan Bible Publishers.

98   97   96   95   94   93   92   91
8   7   6   5   4   3   2   1

CONTENTS

INTRODUCTION

I knew I was going to like Jenny the moment she stepped through the office door and cast a quick, almost suspicious glance around the room. Her demeanor was ladylike as she took a chair and gently pushed back her soft brown curls. She complained of headaches and unexplained crying spells as well as outbursts of anger that she couldn't seem to stop. She fought back the tears and chided herself for not being a perfect wife, mother, and Christian. With a little gentle questioning, it didn't take long for a story of deep hurt and self-pity to come pouring out.

The problem, as she saw it, was her husband. If there were only some way to help him be what God said he was supposed to be, her life would be all right. She wanted to follow what she understood to be the biblical pattern of a submissive wife, but how did one do that with a passive, nonassertive husband who wouldn't know godly leadership if it shook hands with him? She wanted to be a full-time mother, but he was hinting more strongly every day that she should return to work. She wanted a strong Christian father for her children, but Ted had never once sat down with them and opened a Bible. He could find time to go on a fishing trip with a six-pack of beer and his friends, but she and the children could never be worked into his schedule.

I listened for nearly an hour, and when she cried it touched my heart. At the end of the session, I made a few suggestions for relieving a bit of the immediate pain and asked her to make an appointment for the next week. I was fairly sure that she would leave the session feeling much better and thinking of me as a wonderful counselor, but her relief would not have come from anything magical or smart that I had done. I simply had listened to her tell her painful story. For the moment, that was enough.

Alone again in the office, I began to organize the case notes for Jenny's file and thought how easy it would be to lose my counselor's objectivity and become so close to Jenny that I couldn't help her. Little wonder. She reminded me so much of a hurting, young mother I had known quite well a long time ago. She reminded me of me.

During our interview Jenny mentioned that lately "dumb things" had been making her cry. When her children came home from school last week and clicked on an old rerun of "Little House on the Prairie," she had to leave the room when the theme song began. She was overwhelmed by feelings of sadness and grief and ran from the room rather than try to tell her children why Mama was crying.

I did not find Jenny's reaction to the TV program unusual. It was a story I had heard many times before. Some women are confused by sudden flashes of anger brought on by nothing or by a sudden, deep sense of hopelessness that seems to come from nowhere. Jenny's experience of deep grief over silly things is fairly common.

There can be many reasons for seemingly unexplained mood swings. Everything from PMS to depression or a dozen other disorders could be the source of the trouble.

But what I often find in women who are otherwise

healthy and well adjusted is that tears prompted by "small, silly" things are often connected to an unresolved grieving process.

It may involve a woman's loss of her childhood when she was forced to perform as an adult and take over the mother role for her younger siblings; perhaps the real mother of the family was out looking for her drunk husband. Or it may be the loss of what she thought would be an ideal Christian home when, as an adult, her husband left town with his secretary. Often, it will be a painful loss involving a husband, father, or pastor who did not live up to what she knew he should have been.

Whatever the source of the loss, it will have produced a hurt so deep that the woman pushed it to the background and never completed the full cycle of grieving. She dried her tears (often judging tears as something that were helpless to change the situation anyway) and got on with life. Yet the tears were always there just below the surface. When the pressure was strong enough, they splashed over the edge at "silly" provocation.

In my own experience, there had been many triggers that shook my soul enough to make the tears splash out. The one I remember most clearly was a Christmas card that arrived at our home about twenty-five years ago. We were farmers at the time, trying to hold a family together when the economic odds were against us.

It was just an ordinary Christmas card. It had arrived that year along with a few dozen others from friends and relatives, and, of course, one from every business in town to whom we owed money. Like all the rest, it clung to the wall by a short strip of cellophane tape and moved in the breeze when someone passed.

But this card was different because of the unexplained and almost unbearable sadness it stirred in me every time I dared to look at it.

The colored picture on the front showed a living room window in an old, Victorian home. The snow outside the window was accented with glitter. Through the window one could see a parlor dressed with all the trimmings of Christmas and a family gathered around the tree. Bitter cold snow lay on the ground outside the home, but inside the window all was safe and warm. Father sat in a wingback chair. He was wearing a smoking jacket, and a large book was open on his lap. Two children sat on the floor by his feet. They were looking up at their father with faces that beamed with respect and admiration. Mother sat on the sofa. Her hands were busy knitting, and she wore a pink gown.

For several days I studied the card in stolen moments when I thought no one was watching and asked myself why such a simple Christmas card should make me feel so hurt and alone. Then slowly I began to see the answer. The card was a clear picture of the one thing I wanted most in life—the one thing I felt I had never really been able to touch. It was a home with a godly father leading his family and making them secure in his love and provision.

That was something I had never experienced no matter how hard I reached for it. Not in childhood. Not as an adult. When I looked at the card, I felt as though I were standing outside that window with my feet in the snow and my face pressed against the cold glass. It seemed as though I had spent my entire life standing in the snow, wanting to join that family. But I was never able to get inside because there was only one key to the door, and God had not given it to me. God had handed the key to the men in my life, and I was forced to wait in the snow.

When I was a child, the key was given to my dad. Daddy became the town drunk. When I became an adult, the key had been given to my husband. Bill was a Christian, but he wasn't what I thought a true Christian leader should be. He didn't lead his family in daily devotions. His church attendance was inconsistent. He seemed bored with God. When I wanted to talk theology, he was much more interested in the prices on the cattle market.

For me the unresolved grieving process centered around the men in my life who were always, in my opinion, falling short of what I needed them to be. Yet something deep inside me said it was not just my opinion, but God's opinion, too. According to His Word, they were far from what He wanted them to be.

Things would have been so different for me if these men had only shaped up. I felt helpless and alone and angry. But experience had taught me that tears were useless to change the situation, so I pushed them deep inside and went on with a gray, cold life.

Part of me was also very angry with God. As a woman, I felt cheated. I served Him with all my heart, but He gave the keys to my happiness to men and consigned me to stand in the snow and wait for them to get their acts together and rescue me. It was a long, cold wait.

If you are a woman who can identify with the feeling of standing in the snow outside that window, this book is for you. You may be a single woman who has never married or a single mother trying to raise your children alone. You may be married to a non-Christian mate. Perhaps your situation is that you are temporarily alone because your man is off in the armed services. Or your husband is out on the road conducting revivals. He is very busy meeting everyone else's needs while you sit home alone with a crying baby and a washing machine that won't work.

Your struggle may not be with your husband. It could be your grief is over a father who abandoned you long ago; his memory still drags on your life today like a sack of wet sand tied to your heart. You may be married to an alcoholic or a workaholic or a football-aholic.

But whatever your situation, you have this one thing in common with all your other sisters who are standing in the snow: You are in pain, and it seems that a man is at the heart of the problem.

One thing you should know before reading this book is that I am not against men. I like men. Although I have been a widow for the past twelve years, there are still a few men in my life. I almost never date, but I have two grown sons and two sons-in-law. As you read, please remember that I was married for almost twenty years to one of those creatures who grow hair on their faces, and overall it was a good experience. In my current position, I work daily with many different men at all levels of spiritual maturity. I have a great deal of respect for both the male sex and the leadership position God intended for it to fulfill. And I now know that many of the years I stood in the snow resulted from my stubbornness, not from of my husband's failure. Even though Bill has been dead for many years, there are still times when I miss him.

This book is not about rights and principles and ideals. It is about practical, daily living. It seeks to speak to the pain women experience when they feel their leader isn't going anywhere and to make some sense out of Paul's writings on submission when there is no one around to whom a woman can submit. It is written to any woman who has spent time standing outside that window with her feet in the snow to encourage her to hope that God really molded two keys to that closed door and slipped one into her own pocket.

ONE
WHY DO I KEEP

STANDING BY

THE WINDOW?

Some fair questions to ask any woman who has her feet in the snow and her nose pressed against the window are: Why do you keep standing there? Why can't you just forget the whole mess and walk away? Why is it so important to join the family behind the glass? Why do you want a man to fill your dreams? Why not just forget the male sex all together? Life would certainly be a lot simpler if you did.

Indeed, there are those females who believe they have accomplished that very deed. They would tell you that a husband and a home have become optional in their lives. Men and homes are no longer a need with them but simply a little spice that they can take or leave as they choose.

However, women who are more honest and know themselves at a deeper level will usually admit that while they wish men were optional, something deep inside keeps drawing them to the ideal of a little cottage with a white picket fence, a rambling red rose by the front door, and a strong, dominant man coming home to them at sunset.

Walking away from the window is not as easy as it sounds. A woman can tell her heart, "Forget it." But there is no guarantee that it will obey. For most women there is something as strong as life that pulls them back to the window time and time again. It is central to a woman's nature to long to share a home that she has created with a strong, protective man.

One staunch feminist who suddenly found herself slapped with the reality of her own need for male leadership and traditional home life was Colette Dowling.

THE LONGING FEMININE HEART

Colette had been through a divorce, then as a single mother she experienced several years of moderate success in the publishing field. In time she and her children moved in with her boyfriend who was a fellow author, and housekeeping became a joint effort. As the relationship progressed, Ms. Dowling found the structure of her days changing. She no longer spent large amounts of time behind her typewriter but instead was busy cooking and gardening and performing the other necessary chores of homemaking.

According to her own testimony, Colette was happier than she had ever been, but her live-in lover quickly objected to the change he saw in her. If they were going to have a joint relationship, he wanted it to be *totally* joint. Why had she stopped working? Why didn't she get busy and pay her half of the bills?

Her lover's objection to her new life-style shocked Colette. After all, she was pulling her share of the load by turning their house into a home. She still pecked at the typewriter occasionally, and it was not her fault if the publishers no longer wanted her proposals. Her stress over the situation led to panic attacks and finally to psychotherapy.

But an even bigger shock slapped her in the face when she got into therapy and discovered her own hidden feelings. Deep down she *wanted* a man to provide financially for her while she devoted her energy to full-time homemaking. She *wanted* the security of his protection. Something inside her was content to rest in his shadow. Somehow that dependent, supportive, old-fashioned arrangement of a man providing and a woman making a home seemed right and natural and safe.

That realization was almost intolerable to Colette. She was a feminist product of the sixties and seventies. She had always thought of herself as arrogant and aggressive and, above all, independent. She had been the sole support of herself and three children following her divorce. Equality between the sexes had been her marching theme. So why at the core of her being was there a desire that called her away from the job market and toward the kitchen?

Colette turned her writing talent toward this personal problem and began researching the subject for possible publication. Her research uncovered yet another shock. Colette's problem was not an isolated case! She found much psychological research that indicated the vast majority of women had this same "problem." Many of these women had personal income in the six-figure bracket and were "liberated" enough to live with a man or live alone if they wished. These were women who had proven they could rule both the roost and the rooster. They were women others could admire and look up to for having it all.

Yet deep inside these women were struggling with the same difficulties that Colette fought. Deep inside them there was a secret longing to live happily ever after with a strong man who would care for them and help them build a home. At the core of their being, these women wanted the protection, shelter, and care of a man in leadership.

These statistics made Colette really angry. Before she had only been mad at herself for this "weakness" toward men. Now she was mad at all humankind in general. How could this happen after so many years of feminist struggle? What was wrong with women? Didn't they see the value of being free from the oppressive domination of men? Why couldn't they cut that nesting instinct out of their breast, trample it in the dust, and reach for independence?

By this time, publishers were agreeing with Ms. Dowling that she had indeed uncovered the next and perhaps last step in the progress of the feminist movement. With their support, Colette produced her bestseller, *The Cinderella Complex: Woman's Hidden Fear of Independence.* In this book, Colette exposed what she believed to be the "problem" and gave her suggestions for a solution.

She believed that a woman's need for the shelter and protection of a man was not natural. Consequently, she reasoned, it must have been caused by society. Society had trained girls to believe that daddies were supposed to provide security and mothers were supposed to build a comfortable nest for the family. This error in training was what caused the trouble. The "solution" to this "problem" would be to start with a new generation of baby girls and force them from day one to be as independent and self-sufficient as possible. The little girls had to learn to rip out those gentle feelings that told them that turning a house into a home was an honorable occupation. They had to learn to deny the idea that it was noble for a woman to give her life in support

of the success of her man and her children. The,
be taught how to stand alone in a dog-eat-dog world.

I smiled when I read Ms. Dowling's book shortly after
its publication in 1983. She was a crusader bent on victory who was sure she could pry from all women's hearts
the desire for a strong husband and home. She was confident she would win. I was confident she would fail.

Wanting to be cared for by a loving man and to create
a home for him is not a goal that has been trained into
females and imposed on their collective psyche by an
old-fashioned society. The feminine desire for husband
and home has far deeper roots. It is something God
gave Eve.

BACK TO EDEN

I believe that this longing began when paradise was
shattered by sin and God told Eve, "Your desire shall be
to your husband."

At the moment innocence was gone, the world
changed. Because of sin, God cursed the snake. God
cursed the land, too. But when God came to mankind,
what He said is not identified in the Bible as a "curse."
Instead, God simply told the man and woman how different life would be in this new and frightening age that
they, themselves, had begun.

Adam listened as God told him that one of the differences would be that he would now have to sweat and
struggle to earn his daily food. Adam had worked
before—it had always been his job to keep the garden—
but it had been an activity of joy and ease. Now it
would become a burden.

Eve's life would be different, too. From that fateful
moment, things would fill her life that had not been a
part of God's original creation. Eve listened as God told

her of three things that would be different about this strange, new world she had opened. One, God would increase her pain in childbirth. Two, she would have a desire for her husband. And three, her husband would rule over her.

All three of God's statements to Eve are important because they still affect our lives today. Just as pain in childbirth was something not only she would experience but also her daughters for all generations would know, even so God's other two statements would affect women through the ages. We will cover God's third statement—that men would rule over women—in chapter 2, and God's first statement about pain in childbirth will be examined in chapter 10. For this chapter I would like to look at the second statement, the one that concerns Eve's heart.

ONE POINT OF VIEW

God told Eve, "Your desire will be for your husband, and he will rule over you" (Genesis 3:16, NIV). There are only two other places where this form of "desire" (i.e., longing) is used in the Bible. One is in Song of Songs 7:10 where the bride makes the statement about her groom, "I belong to my lover, and his *desire* is for me" (NIV, italics added).

The other place is in the discourse between God and Cain in Genesis 4:7. In this reference, as in Genesis 3:16, "desire" and "rule" are placed together. Although the verbs in both verses are exactly the same in the original language, the New International Version of the Bible translates God's words to Cain as: "But if you do not do what is right, sin is crouching at your door; it *desires* to have you but you must *master* it" (Genesis 4:7, italics added).

Because of this similarity, some scholars see a reflection between the struggle Cain would have with mastering sin and the struggle Eve would have as she tried to master Adam. In other words, this was the opening shot in the battle of the sexes in which Eve would try to wrest the leadership from Adam. But in the end she would fail, and he would rule her instead.

I am somewhat cautious about taking a different stand from this view that is widely held and backed by conservative scholars. However, I feel like Jeremiah, who thought he would pop if he didn't speak what was on his heart (Jeremiah 20:9).

I don't doubt that there is a battle going on between the sexes as each tries to dominate the other, but I do question whether this battle was initiated by God and whether it is a unique struggle between male and female. The contest to see who can win the title of top dog goes on in every relationship. Unless two individuals are very mature and have spent years growing in Christ, there will almost always be a hint of competition mixed with pride between them. Mother and daughter, parent and child, boss and worker, husband and wife—all have times of struggle for dominance. This is such a common phenomenon that whole theories of psychology have been built on it.

The marriage relationship is one of the most intimate. It is not surprising that the struggle for control is often acute in such closeness. But this battle is not a peculiarity of a war between male and female. It is a continuation of the common war that is raging all around us. It has little to do with the woman as a female, but it has everything to do with all humans as flesh.

Another problem with believing that this part of the verse refers to the beginning of the age-old battle of the sexes is that our struggle for dominance and control of each other is a sin of the flesh nature. Working by the sweat of Adam's brow was not a sin. Pain in childbirth was not a sin. Why would God give Eve a sinful struggle for control that would dominate her relationship with her husband all her earthly life?

THE WAY I SEE IT

When God told Eve, "your desire shall be to your husband," it reflected God's decision to place in Eve the emotional need for husband and home. This statement is not about Eve's war, but about Eve's heart. God's three statements to Eve are about things that are unique to women. He is telling her about her new life outside the garden and how it will be different from the life she has known before and different from the life of Adam as well.

When God told Eve that her desire would now be toward her husband, He was indicating a change in her needs. She was going to desire, want, and long for her husband in a different way. This was the beginning of that urgency inside a woman that draws her toward her husband and home. And it is that desire and longing that keeps a lot of women in the snow. This desire is not a bad thing or a sin, but like all other desires, it must be brought under the Lordship of Jesus if it is to stay a desire rather than growing into a need-driven addiction.

This instinct is not present in men in the same way it is in women. It is the woman that is likely to start hearing wedding bells after the second date. It is the woman who starts a hope chest and begins packing away little things for her future home long before she actually needs pots and dishes.

Of course, there are exceptions to this for both male and female, but these individuals are few. For proof just take a look at any grocery-store magazine rack. There are several magazines devoted strictly to brides, but I know of none on the market for grooms. A woman's heart turns toward husband and home while she is still very young, and no amount of new social training will change it.

Frankly, I think it is good that God gave us this desire for husband and home. If He had not, the human race might have died out long ago. Although women have a desire for home and a dependence that draws them toward marriage, if marriage does not occur, women do quite well alone. Statistically, women appear to get along without men far better than men get along without women. A man who never marries will probably die young, but an unmarried woman will likely outlive her married counterpart. Widows make a better adjustment to living alone than do widowers.

If this ability to live without men were not balanced with a desire that drew women toward the home and male leadership, I doubt that sexual need alone would have been enough to propel the continuation of the race. Considering many men's tendency to become overbearing and a woman's need to give sex only in a relationship of love and mutual caring, the two sexes might have gone their separate ways.

THE PRACTICAL SIDE

So far this chapter has been a description of the problem and Bible theory. I suspect some of my readers may be getting pretty frustrated about this time. You may feel you already know the problem, and you invested in this book to find answers! Well, there really are answers, but they only make sense when we have a biblical foundation on which to lay them and a working knowledge of the exact problem.

One practical way we can use this biblical insight involves our self-image. If we know that God has created in us a desire for husband and home, then we don't have to be ashamed of those feelings or fight them or consider ourselves unusual when they boil up strong and painful. The tears and the longing become a natural desire that—like other desires—must not become the central driving force in our lives, but a piece of living that can add richness when it remains under the control of the Spirit.

When we realize this desire is from God and is meant for our good, we have hope that the One who gave the desire will have no difficulty filling it. That may seem an impossible dream to the woman stuck in the snow, because filling that desire is something she has likely spent years struggling with, and, as far as she can tell, God has never answered her prayer.

The psalmist asked the question, "Does he who implanted the ear not hear? Does he who formed the eye not see?" (Psalm 94:9, NIV). We might reframe the question for the woman in the snow and ask, "Does the One who created the need for male leadership and home in a woman's heart not know how to fill it?"

Surely, the One who put an ear on the side of the head knows how to hear, and the One who molded the complex mechanism of the eye knows how to see. It is just as certain that the One who created each need in a woman's heart also knows how to fill those needs. The only mystery is how the filling is to be accomplished.

God always fills all our needs, but the way He fills them is sometimes very curious and unexpected. For example, take such a basic need as our need for food. God created people with a need to eat. At first that need was supplied without effort on man's part. Food was abundant for the picking.

When sin entered the world, the process changed, but people still had the need to eat and God still made the provision. Now food would be supplied through hard work. Adam would dig in the ground and plant. God would make it grow. Adam would harvest and store, and the daily cycle of hunger would be satisfied. This has ever since been the normal, natural way that God has ordained for our natural hunger needs to be met.

But when Israel left Egypt, the normal means of hunger satisfaction was not available. God had between one and three million people caught in a sand desert. There was no soil to grow food, no rain to water it, and no time to sit still and wait for it to grow. In this situation, God did not sit around wringing His hands and worrying because the normal path to need satisfaction was blocked. God simply bypassed the normal and went straight to the miraculous. He spread food on the ground each morning that melted when the sun was hot. His children called it *manna*, which in their language meant, "What is it?"

This strange food looked like little beads or seeds. It was hard and could be ground, and when baked it tasted like fine flour mixed with a little honey. It could be cooked in a number of different ways, but only stayed fresh for twenty-four hours. Each morning there was a new supply of manna on the ground. Any way one might consider it, manna was strange stuff. It was odd. It was different. God chose an unnatural way to fill the natural hunger need that He, Himself, had placed inside His people.

When considering a woman's natural need for a strong husband and a secure home, the normal, natural means for that need to be satisfied is through the love of a godly husband. That is the way the system is designed to work. That is the New Testament pattern. This natural means of need satisfaction involves much time and work, just as the natural means of hunger satisfaction demands those things.

Yet, there are times when the normal way is not available. The need is still present in a woman's heart, but the obvious means to fill that need is an impossibility. Perhaps the woman's husband has left her and the children for another woman; or he seems determined to remain an alcoholic; or the woman is single simply because she never found a dedicated, Christian man to marry; or her husband is dead. There can be a thousand reasons why her need for a husband who is a strong leader cannot be filled in the normal way. It is at those times that God often steps in with an alternate means of need fulfillment that can take us by surprise.

When God begins to work in unusual ways, His options are so creative and varied that it is impossible to list them. What He chooses to fill the need of one individual may be totally different from what He chooses for another. One woman may never find a husband, but she may find her need for family and home met as she shelters dozens of orphans for which no one else will care. Another woman may build a secure, happy home as a single parent and be so successful that the absent father is only a small part of their lives.

A woman may find various personal and family needs met by members of her extended family or her church family. My own widowed mother is a secretary for an unusually close-knit church. She believes the pastors and elders she works for are part of God's fulfillment of her need for male leadership. From the way they all care for her, I think she is right!

We should not be surprised at these provisions. God sometimes dealt with the need of hunger by simply eliminating it for a while. He did that, for instance, when Moses was on the mountain without food or water for forty days but suffered no ill effects. The One who created the need can certainly take the need away if He chooses.

THE REST OF THE STORY

I would like to say that all the woman in the snow has to do when she is feeling the ache of that deep, empty need that God placed inside her is to look around and find God's alternate means of need satisfaction and then live happily ever after. I would like to say that . . . but I can't, because it is not true.

God does have many ways of satisfying our needs; however, total need satisfaction is not guaranteed in this present evil age. God is more interested in our growth than in our comfort. Sometimes His answers to our needs can take tears and time. We need to remain open to His alternate means of need satisfaction and willing to let Him eliminate the need if He should choose. But, oh, how we are stretched as we wait for His provision!

That is not what the woman in the snow wants to hear. The children are growing and they need a dad. Her own heart is hurting and the years are passing. Where is God? Where is the answer? She pleads, "Lord, I put a rush ticket on this prayer two years ago! What happened? Did it get lost in transit, or is there some reason You are mad at me?"

It can be very hard to wait on God, and when He answers in a way we were not expecting, we sometimes feel cheated or abandoned by the One we thought would never fail us. We not only want our prayers answered, we want them answered in the way we requested! We may find ourselves like the Old Testament prophet Habakkuk, who spent the first half of his little book pleading, "God, why don't You do something about this mess?" and the last half lamenting, "No, Lord, I didn't mean for You to fix it *that* way!"

But Habakkuk found his answer in the end, and at the conclusion of his work he states that no matter how crazy the situation might become and no matter how impossible natural need satisfaction might seem to the logical mind, he would continue to rejoice in the Lord. He would believe that God is his strength and trust that through it all God would teach him to walk in power on the high places (Habakkuk 3:17-19).

God placed in Eve's daughters a need for husband and home. He may provide for that need through natural means or through unusual means. Or He may choose to let the need go empty for a time while He develops our character and our patience. He may even develop our joy as we learn to live above our circumstances and not under them. He works in His own time and His own way. Our job is just to keep trusting.

There will come a day when all need is ultimately satisfied. We call it "heaven." But until that day we live by faith and not by sight. We travel in a land that is sometimes barren and difficult. Our needs are real, but dear sister in Christ, rest contented, for His provision for those needs is real also.

> The Lord will guide you always; he will satisfy your needs in a sun-scorched land. (Isaiah 58:11, NIV)

TWO

WHY DID GOD

CHOOSE MEN

TO LEAD?

Often when teaching a group of women, I ask those
who feel they have a poor self-image to raise their
hands. I always take care to set the stage for this question by encouraging them to think positively. Yet when
hands go up, between 75 and 100 percent of the
women in the room will indicate they believe they have
a basically poor self-image. It amazes me.

Why such an extensive negative self-report? Could it
be simply a fashionable craze to say one has low self-
image? Could it be that many Christians feel that giving
one's self a bad report is a sign of humility? Where did
women get all these negative feelings?

The answers to these questions would fill many
books. Our own expectations, societal demands, childhood upbringing, the changing role of women—these
and other factors have all had their influence. But one
of the strangest sources of self-condemnation that I see
in my office is a belief that the Bible teaches women are
second-class citizens. They are not quite worthy simply
because they are women and not men.

This idea is not usually expressed in the first meeting with a client, but as she begins to feel the office is a safe place and gets in touch with her own anger or grief, the question comes to the surface: Why did God choose men to lead? When a woman loves God so much, why did He choose men to head both the home and the church? What was wrong with her that God passed her over and picked a man?

I can sympathize with this question. In fact, I have agonized over it. For many years it was a painful sore that never quite healed no matter how much I grew in spiritual maturity. It seemed so illogical for God to pass over women and hand the leadership to men.

On any typical Sunday in Averagetown, U.S.A., the women gathered in various church congregations will outnumber the men two to one. In the choir the ratio is often three to one, and among church school teachers it may jump to something like five to one. For several years I served on the nominating committee for a small church, and I became very weary of asking men to do things and having them turn me down. It seemed as if when I asked the average male church member to take a responsibility in the local church, he would look at me as though I had just asked him to donate his teeth to a worthy cause. I finally resigned.

I don't mean to indicate by this chapter that there are no godly men. Of course, there are—thousands of them! Men are pastors and counselors and song leaders and education directors in churches all over the country. There are men lay leaders in most all congregations, and many men lead their homes in the things of God.

But these leaders are vastly outnumbered by Christian women who pray and teach Sunday school and go to church alone. Multiplied thousands of women are holding together the spiritual life of their home, and they often form the backbone of the local church as well. These women dress the children, drive to church, and sit on a pew Sunday after Sunday while Papa stays home to watch the ball game or sleep late.

When we take these facts that we see all around us every week and hold them up beside the fact that God chose men to be leaders in the home, it is no wonder that women get confused and question God. They feel as though God is unfair because it seems He is partial to men or has given women some deep flaw that makes them unfit for leadership.

For myself, I've never had a problem believing in male leadership. When my husband and I married, I checked our vows to make sure mine would include the word *obey.* I find myself not so much resenting the fact that men were chosen to be leaders as feeling frustrated over *why* they were chosen. Women are such a sensitive, noble breed; why didn't God place the leadership of the home and the church into their tender hands? Why did God choose men?

I knew God was bound to have had some reason for His action. The universe is too precisely balanced to believe that He took a cosmic gamble on blind chance. I could not imagine Him looking at Adam and Eve and saying, "There can't be two leaders. Someone has got to follow, so one of you choose heads and one of you choose tails, and we will flip this mule and see which end comes out on top." But if God was not acting on chance, what was His reasoning?

For any woman who is either spiritually or physically alone, the question of why God chose men to lead becomes very important. She has got to know what God was trying to accomplish through that choice before she can apply it to her own life. Also, if a woman never understands why God chose men, she can easily build a deep resentment and anger toward both God and men because she feels they put her down and demean her without cause.

My curiosity about this subject drove me from one commentary to another and to several different respected pastors. I got very little in the way of results. No matter what library I searched or who I asked, information on this subject was scant to nonexistent.

Finally, an acquaintance who served many years on the staff of Dallas Theological Seminary suggested that the root of the problem was that commentaries and books were written almost exclusively by men. It had never occurred to them to question why they were chosen!

That seemed logical. But I was a woman, and I did ask the question. I asked it a lot. It bugged me. Why? Why did God choose men to be leaders?

After many years of head scratching and prayer, I think I may have a few ideas on this subject. I would like to take this chapter to share them with you.

IN SEARCH OF A REASON

At times God lets us in on what He is thinking and gives us clear reasons for what He does. For example, concerning Christ's coming into the world, the Bible explains, "For God so loved the world, that he gave his only begotten Son" (John 3:16). Why did God allow Jesus to come? Because He loved the world. We know the why behind God's action.

But at other times God's reasons are less clear. On these occasions we must fall back on other resources—God's character and the principles and reasoning He has left us in the Word. We become somewhat like detectives searching for valid clues and piecing together possibilities. When we have a lot of clues that all lead to the same conclusion, we can put our theological feet down with a fair bit of certainty. I believe that the search for the reasons God chose men for leadership falls into this category.

However, before we begin looking for clues, let me note that the Bible makes it clear what some of God's reasons were *not.* God did not feel that males were somehow more noble or less sinful than females. Death and sin enter each generation through the male, not the female (Romans 5:12; 1 Corinthians 15:21-22). Many scholars believe this is why it was necessary for Jesus to be born of a virgin.

Also, when God looks at mankind, He sees humans, not males and females (Galatians 3:28). In fact, when God created the first man and woman, He gave them one name between them. God didn't give the woman the name of Eve; Adam gave her that name. God only had one name for both his creatures, "Adam" in Hebrew (Genesis 5:2). Her name was Adam as well as his.

God does not value men more than women. Just because He chose one sex to rule over the other does not mean that He rejoices in the greatness of the one and discards the other. I voted last election for a candidate in the Texas governor's race, but it wasn't much fun. It was a choice of bad or worse. God must have felt a bit like that when He was faced with the problem of establishing a government for the home. He needed a leader for the job, but neither candidate was worth much consideration. They were a pair of losers dressed in tattered fig leaves, each accusing the other of being the cause of their downfall.

But God did make His choice (Genesis 3:16). I believe

that a careful study of the principles and indications of the Word will build a fairly good case to show that He chose men because women, while more spiritually sensitive, are less discerning.

WOMEN ARE MORE SPIRITUALLY SENSITIVE

The spiritual sensitivity of women is evident both in the Bible and by a good look at our own society. One can pick almost any congregation of almost any denomination in almost any town in our land, and when the skirts and pants are counted, skirts will take the prize almost every time. The women will dominate in attendance.

Occasionally, this overpopulation of females has given the Christian church the undeserved reputation of being an organization designed for women and children. It is sometimes regarded as a sewing circle which real, macho men don't take seriously.

Even in the New Testament there was a problem created because women responded to the gospel and their husbands did not. In his letter, which was to be circulated throughout the churches of the Near East, Peter gave specific instructions to women who were married to unbelieving men (1 Peter 3:1-6). However, he offered no such instructions for men married to unbelieving wives. It is likely there were some mixed marriages where the man was a Christian and the woman was not, just as there are marriages like that today, but it was not such a large problem that the apostle felt it needed special attention in a general letter to many churches. The problem of women married to unbelieving men was of general concern.

Something in the nature of women makes them more open and curious about spiritual things. It is as though Eve walked out of Eden with a special tenderness in her heart that still remains in her daughters today. But before we get too proud, remember that individual women can also lose spiritual sensitivity and become more hard than any man ever dared. Just because something is true of the general population does not make it necessarily true of the individual. Women can become as heartless and cold as Athaliah as she moved through the palace killing her own grandchildren in order to secure the throne for herself (2 Kings 11:1).

Our spiritual sensitivity is not always something of which to brag. Spiritual tenderness can cause problems. Just as the local Christian church has women as its main base, so do many of the corrupt religions of the world. Anything spiritual will draw more women than men. When someone mentions the word *medium*, most of us think of a woman with a crystal ball even though a man can be a medium, too. Witchcraft, voodoo, spirit worship, fortune telling, and astrology are all dominated by females.

It seems that women are blessed with a special sensitivity to spiritual things that men often lack. Just as an animal can pick up high-frequency sounds that are unheard by human ears, a woman can sense the presence of the spiritual realm while a man goes about his business unaware. She can feel the pull of the spiritual world and hear the call of the supernatural far more easily than he can.

But a serious problem is created because she is less spiritually discerning. She is drawn to the spiritual, but she can have a dreadful time figuring out which spirits, teachings, impressions, and feelings are from heaven and which are from hell.

WOMEN ARE LESS SPIRITUALLY DISCERNING

It is easy to say that women are less spiritually discerning and to point to social examples for proof, but can
such a statement be backed up by Scripture? I believe it
can.

However, we have to do careful detective work. The
Bible never says outright that women have a problem
with spiritual discernment. But I believe we can infer
this when we look at the restrictions and warnings that
the New Testament writers directed only to women.

The first clue we will examine is that famous phrase
of the apostle Paul's that might have won him the title
of "Male Chauvinist Pig of the Year" were he our con-
temporary. He said, "Let your women keep silence in
the churches" (1 Corinthians 14:34).

Oh, groan! What pain and confusion those eight little
words have caused! What strange interpretations they
have occasionally sparked!

I have read explanations of this verse that range from
accusing the ladies of having bad manners and talking
out loud during church services to guessing that the
women wore bangle bracelets that jingled loudly when
they moved! Some have suggested that these verses
mean women can do anything but preach; others say
they can do anything but talk in tongues; and still
others simply state that Paul was speaking from his
own cultural setting and modern congregations can
ignore him!

We know that Paul was not referring to all noise or all
speaking in all circumstances. If that were the case, he
would be contradicting himself because only three
chapters back he told the Corinthians that all members
of the congregation were free to pray and prophesy
(1 Corinthians 11:52), and we know that women were
prophets as well as men (Acts 21:9). One can't prophesy

without speaking! When we let Scripture interpret Scripture, we know that in these verses Paul was bound to be referring to a certain kind of speaking that was forbidden to women. But that begs the question: What kind of speaking?

If we look back only two sentences from Paul's admonition in 1 Corinthians 14:34, we find he instructed, "The spirits of prophets are subject to the control of prophets" (verse 32, NIV). I believe a woman is told to keep silent in this public control that the prophets exercised over each other.

The services of the early church were much different in format than those of most modern denominations. Our hymn singing, offering, special music, sermon, invitation and/or benediction would be totally foreign to those early believers. Their services involved much more spontaneity. Meetings were held in large homes or public lecture halls or outdoors or sometimes in synagogues. Music could be given by most anyone at most any time or by everyone in unison. Several believers spoke at each meeting. In fact, Paul had to correct the Corinthians because speakers were often talking at the same time.

Can you imagine the confusion when one speaker was going full steam at the front of the room and two more were shouting Old Testament Scripture at the back? Paul said everyone should be allowed to speak (including women), but they should do so only one at a time (1 Corinthians 14:29-31).

In the early church, the only Scripture available was the Old Testament, and this was in very limited supply. Many in the congregation were from the slave class or the working poor and could not read. Qualified teachers were in short supply, and false teachers were an ever-present threat to the fledgling church. One of the most important tests they faced was how to keep communication between God and the church pure and authoritative.

Part of their system of quality control was a series of checks and balances. As individual prophets spoke to the congregation, their words were weighed by the other prophets present in the service. It was the job of these fellow prophets to keep wrong teaching out and to judge whether or not the prophet who was speaking was indeed sharing a message from God or, perhaps, a message from the devil.

Imagine yourself as a woman prophet sitting three rows from the back of the room on a summer Sunday morning. Worship and praise and singing and speaking has been going on for about an hour and a half when brother John Doe rises and says he has a word from the Lord. He states that the Lord has told him that the congregation of believers in Salamis will be facing financial difficulty in the next year. He says the Lord would have the church collect a large offering to be sent to Salamis and distributed to the widows and orphans of that congregation.

You don't really want to call John a liar. However, you know that his sister lives in Salamis with her six kids and that she was recently widowed. You wonder how much of John's message is coming from the Lord and how much is coming from John's unwillingness to face his personal responsibility to help his sister in her distress.

What should you do? Should you stand up and tell that you think John has made a mistake? You feel in your spirit that the Lord is telling you that John is wrong, but are you right? You know the Lord would not be telling you one thing and John something else.

I believe this is the type of situation that prompted

Paul's instruction that a woman keep silent in the church. This is the type of speaking that a woman is not to do publicly. She is not to openly judge whether a fellow prophet or prophetess has heard from the Lord or not. She is not to publicly judge the spiritual source of another prophet's statement until she has first given the matter time and checked it out through a man, preferably her husband. If she still has deep doubts about the validity of John's prophetic message, she can ask her husband what he thought about it. Did John hear from the Lord? Is he telling the congregation a true prophecy? If her husband agrees that correction needs to be made, it can be handled privately and not by a woman before the church.

This is one example of where a restriction is placed on women but not on men. I believe that restriction indicates that women, in general, are less able to identify the source of spiritual impulses.

Another Scripture that indicates women may have a problem with spiritual discernment is 2 Timothy 3:6. Again, Paul gave instructions. This time he warned the church about false teachers. He really jumped on them in this passage. When describing false teachers he claimed they "creep into houses, and lead captive silly women laden with sins, led away with divers lusts."

For years that passage really set my teeth on edge. Why didn't Paul say "silly men"? The New International Version translates that Scripture as "weak-willed" women, and the New King James Version says "gullible." But no matter what translation one picks up, the painting is not flattering to the female sex!

Now I know there are silly women in this world, but some men are real dingbats, too! And, as for being "laden with sins" or "led away with lust," it seems to me that the male sex has us ladies beat by a mile! Why did Paul pick out silly women to be connected with false teachers? I believe this is another example indicating that women by nature have a problem with spiritual discernment.

One word of warning: Don't presume too much on one passage of Scripture without looking at the whole. Paul does not say that all women, no matter how long they have been walking with the Lord, are always spiritually stupid, gullible, silly, and weak willed. The writer of Hebrews notes that any Christian can develop a maturity that causes him or her to distinguish good from evil (Hebrews 5:14), and the Holy Spirit can bestow a special gift on both men and women that makes them particularly sensitive to the sources of spiritual teaching and impulse (1 Corinthians 12:10). But Paul was speaking generally to Timothy about what he would most likely find in his large congregation: The women would be the first to be led astray by false teachers.

A third place where the tendency of women in general to have trouble with spiritual discernment is found in 1 Timothy 2:11-12: "Let the woman learn in silence with all subjection. But I suffer not a woman to teach, nor to usurp authority over the man."

Paul must have created a king-sized debate in some churches when he opened this passage by stating that women should be taught the things of God. In his day, women were seldom taught the basics of math or reading, much less the deep truths of God! I can just see the eyebrows rise on the older men as their mouths dropped wide open. Bring women into the congregation and teach them doctrine? The idea must have blown their minds! But Paul assured them that the women are to learn with quietness and full submission—just like any other new student should learn.

They would not be there to stir up trouble or start a revolution, but to take their proper places as students.

Next, Paul told Timothy that there is a certain type of teaching that women are not to do. We know Paul was referring to some particular type of teaching and not to all teaching in general, because other Scriptures, many of which Paul himself wrote, indicate places where a woman should teach.

Just as the Corinthian passage we looked at earlier referred to women being silent in certain situations, this passage commands that women not engage in a particular type of teaching. He qualifies this teaching as being a type that would "usurp authority over the man."

This phrase has sparked a lot of hot debate. One of the complications that makes it so difficult is that the entire phrase is only one word in the Greek, and it is a word that is used nowhere else in the Bible. In fact, it is hardly used anywhere else in Greek literature. The closest translators can come is that it is a military term used of officers who had the power of life and death over their troops.

Personally, I am not certain what type of teaching Paul is forbidding women to do through this passage. But one thing is certain: There is *some* type of teaching that Paul does not want women to be involved in, and he said these same instructions were from God and to be used in all the churches.

Paul based his argument for insisting that this type of teaching not be done by women on the fact that Eve fell into sin by being deceived. She thought she was doing the right thing—the logical thing. She reached for what she thought would bring goodness and instead grabbed ahold of death. Eve was not as skilled as Adam in the art of spiritual discernment.

A FINAL WORD

We've seen biblical precedents in three Scriptures: That women were forbidden to judge the spirit from which a fellow prophet spoke (1 Corinthians 14:29-35); that women in general would be the first to be led astray by false teachers (2 Timothy 3:6); and that there were certain kinds of teaching women should not do in the church because Eve (and her daughters) were easily deceived (1 Timothy 2:11-14). These Scriptures are enough to build a case supporting the fact that men were chosen by God for leadership because they have, in general, a better judgment when it comes to determining what is and is not of the devil.

For a moment, think back to Eden and consider God's problem. Sin had entered the world. Humanity already had the stench of death and was rapidly drifting from God. The children God created were caught in a riptide that would carry them farther and farther from His presence. Soon He would no longer be able to communicate with them face to face. As their sin increased, it would clash with God's holiness until finally the strain of seeing God and being near Him would be enough to kill a man (Exodus 33:20). Yet communication with God would be the one vital factor that had to be kept as pure as possible if humanity was to survive on planet Earth.

Without clear communication from God, people would never know His laws and judgments. They would be wild beings searching for laws on their own with no guidance except their personal selfishness. Without communication from God, people would never know that He loved them. They would never know that something lay beyond this life and that hope still existed for a future.

How could God best keep that fragile communication between Himself and humanity flowing unpolluted? Knowing the woman's sensitivity to His voice would easily be spoiled by Satan's lies and tricks and remembering her gullibility, God turned to her and said of her husband, "He shall rule over thee" (Genesis 3:16).

THREE

THE MAN

OF MY DREAMS

An old nursery rhyme asks the question, "What are
little boys made of?" then goes on to give the dubious
answer: "Frogs and snails and puppy dog tails, that's
what little boys are made of." I never did understand
what a dog tail had to do with constructing a boy any
more than I understood the first part of the rhyme that
claimed girls were made out of sugar and spice, but I
remember we girls would shout the rhyme at the boys
when we wanted to show them how worthless they
were. Somehow we assumed that sugar and spice made
better building blocks for personal worth than frogs
and snails!

A lot of human history has passed since some child
first chanted that rhyme. One would think that the two
sexes might have learned more about each other since
then, but I wonder. In any given bookstore one will
likely find a shelf crammed with volumes that attempt
to explain to women why men act like they do, and the
shelf below it will contain just as many volumes
explaining women to men. Yet for all the books and talk
shows and questions, the two sexes still scratch their
heads and wonder what makes the other one tick.

I would like to share with you all that I know about the complex secrets of the male mystique, but if that's all I did, this would be a very short book. Even after being married for twenty years, raising two sons, gaining a graduate degree in the field of psychology, adjusting to two sons-in-law, and dealing with men daily as both professional peers and clients, the male species is still a mystery to me.

This chapter is not about what men are, but about something that is far more important—what we women *think* they are and what we think they *should* be.

THE BUILDING OF A MAN

The old rhyme is biologically on shaky ground, but it does make a good psychological point. We don't build boys out of frogs, but we do build our ideas about them from external sources. In other words, we use outside information, ideas, and examples to form the opinion about men that we hold inside our brains. It is something we learn. We learn it from observation and from what we are told. We learn it from experience and from what we feel. Line by line, lesson by lesson, we learn who we are as females and who they are as males. We determine how males act, think, and feel, and, just as important, we learn what we should expect from them.

Our ideas of who boys are and how they are different from us begin to form in our feminine brains from the moment we are brought protesting into the hospital nursery. The sign over our head reads I Am a Girl, and the one over the head in the bassinet next to ours reads I Am a Boy. Within days, we are dressed in ruffles and wrapped in a pink blanket to go home while the little boy next to us is stuffed into a one-piece suit with a slogan across the front that says Future Dallas Cowboy Quarterback. This is the beginning of a thousand small differences that will teach us how we are different from the opposite sex.

One difference between boys and girls is that from birth people will respond differently to each sex. Psychological researchers are always doing something tricky like dressing a little boy as though he were a girl, introducing him by the name of "Shirley" to some unsuspecting adult, then standing behind a one-way mirror to see how the adult responds to the child. Later, the same child is re-dressed, called "Bill," and given to the same or a different adult. Under careful observation of adult reactions, a pattern soon emerges. Adults, both male and female, will respond differently to each child according to what sex they believe it to be. For example, they tend to talk more to a child they think is a girl and to play more roughly with one they think is a boy. Thus, the male and female halves of humanity take different paths from the starting line.

The learning process that teaches us who we are and who males are is not a conscious effort. Rather, it is something that is caught as we move along through life. We absorb these ideas as naturally as a sponge soaks up water. We learn by watching the example of our parents. We borrow from what we have heard other people say. We observe social norms and take from what we hear in Sunday school. We pick up pieces of information from TV shows and roadside billboards that we pass on the highway. All this information is processed in our minds and pressed through our own value system, and *bingo!* out pops our idea of men.

WHAT MEN *SHOULD* BE

I believe that as we grow from little girls to women, we all develop at least two views of men. The first is about men as we think they should be, and the second, about men as we think they really are.

Our "should be" male is our ideal. I wouldn't go so far as to say he is our Prince Charming, but he comes close. This is the man we could love and respect and submit to without any real problem. He is the model we use when we try to chip away the rough spots in our real mate. It is the misty hope for this ideal man that makes us feel a little cheated when our dream and our reality are viewed side by side.

Each woman will have her own special idea of what men should be. For example, one may believe that men should know how to fix the car. If her man cannot do that, he will be a little less in her eyes. Oh, it probably won't shake the foundations of their marriage, and she may still love him dearly, but she will feel a bit of a twinge that he didn't quite measure up to what she expected of him. To another woman, a man should be romantic. He ought to write love notes, remember special occasions, and surprise her frequently with flowers. If he doesn't do these things—or if he does them only because he knows she wants them—she may be disappointed.

The problem created by these ideals—these *shoulds* and *oughts*—is that they can easily make us discontented with the real, live man who sits across the breakfast table from us. This discontentment will range from a mild uneasiness to an all-out fury and even divorce depending on two factors: how firmly a woman believes the *shoulds* are justified and realistic and how determined she is to make her man fit her ideal image.

One woman may have such strong ideas about every

detail of manhood and be so determined to pound her husband into that mold that she is continually stressed out and angry and feeling very cheated by life for providing her with such a dud for a husband. Across the street, another woman whose husband has very similar faults may feel only a mild discontentment over a few particular things that she believes should be different. But since these things aren't different, she overlooks them and gets on with life.

Although every woman has her own idea of what a man should be and the kind of home and personal satisfaction he should give her, there are a few common ideas that I seem to run across repeatedly. I would like to take the rest of this chapter to look at a few of these. As we go through them, examine your own misty dreams. What have you convinced yourself *should* be part of a Christian husband?

A "NORMAL" CHRISTIAN HOME

One of the most common assumptions Christian women make about men and their role is that somewhere out there in never-never land there exists a thing called a "normal" Christian home. Although this image involves the whole idea of home and not just husband, the husband and our expectations of him are very much a part of this picture. He has got to be what he should be before the home can be what it should be. Often this ideal home looks something like a cross between "Lassie" and "Leave It to Beaver." We draw from our culture, our dreams, and our wants, and we never seriously look into Scripture to determine if our *shoulds* match the examples we find there.

Remember the Christmas card described in the introduction to this book? The one with the strong, silent father in the smoking jacket, the submissive mother dressed in pink, and the two obedient children who all live in the charming Victorian home? That was my idea of normal Christian living. Looking back, I am embarrassed to admit it, but I had so firmly convinced myself that this one picture and nothing else was normal that it took the Lord fifteen years to convince me otherwise.

Clinging stubbornly to that ideal dream nearly ruined my every chance for contentment. When my husband refused to wear pajamas, much less a smoking jacket, and pulled real cigarettes from his pocket; when my four children acted like sons of Adam instead of always being quiet and obedient; when my own personality grew uncomfortable in pink lace; and, most important of all, when my house was a rent-what-you-can instead of Victorian, I was crushed. I felt my home was less than normal. I had been cheated out of a basic standard that all Christian families deserved. It was only with a great deal of difficulty and tears that our Lord convinced me that normal—as I insisted on defining it—was not part of His pattern for me.

When we let the Bible be our guide rather than our personal wants and culture, we will find a great deal of difference among various Christian homes. Peter traveled extensively, and much of this was apparently done with his wife in tow (1 Corinthians 9:5). I don't know what they did with the kids. Timothy's mother raised her son as a spiritual single parent even though she may have had a military husband hanging around somewhere. Philip had a wife and five daughters and lived most of his life in one small town. However, Aquila and Priscilla may have been childless, and they moved all over the map while running a business out of their living room.

All these homes produced great work for the kingdom of God. They were all truly Christian homes, but only the home of Philip came even close to what I had always assumed was "normal."

The men who led these homes were just as full of variety. Peter was impetuous and quick to act. Timothy was reticent. Aquila appears to have been quiet, and his wife may have been the more outspoken of the two, for often her name is listed before his when the couple is referred to in Scripture. The home Timothy grew up in had no godly male leadership at all, but that did not keep it from being a truly Christian home.

Christian homes still come in all shapes and sizes and circumstances. Some are led by forceful men, some are led by quiet men, and some are led by no man at all. Before we start throwing rocks at our man for not providing us with a "normal" Christian home, we need to examine exactly what we are calling "normal." The source for our discontentment may be not so much the fault of our man as the fault of our insistence on using personal definitions and dreams rather than God's examples.

Our homes may have many difficulties that make them less than what we think of as normal Christian homes. The father may be harsh or he may be timid. Illness may make it impossible for one partner to fill his or her role. We may believe there are too many children and not enough money or too much money and no child. Our own lack of maturity and faith may grieve us. We know we fall short of what a godly wife and mother should be. The house may be old and the roof falling in, or our affluent suburban home may be empty and cold.

But none of these conditions or any others will make it impossible for us to call ours a "Christian" home. *All* homes fall short of the perfect ideal in some way, and most homes fall very short at some period in their growth. If we ourselves are Christians, we already have a normal Christian home.

A MAN SHOULD SUPPLY MY HAPPINESS

Sometimes when I suggest to women that they are expecting too much from their husbands, they are surprised and even resentful. A woman has been hurt, cheated, and left without quality leadership. How dare I suggest that she is expecting too much? In fact, she would settle for half as much love, faithfulness, and support as the Scriptures say is ideal.

But sometimes her expectations have nothing to do with what the Scriptures indicate a man should be. A wife may have one expectation that is so high that the only way for her husband to fill it would be if the Holy Trinity became a quartet: She expects him to be the source of all her happiness. Deep down she believes that fairy tales do come true and happiness should come walking into her life dressed in a sport coat and smelling of after-shave.

It isn't any wonder that this belief is so deeply a part of us that we hardly recognize it is sitting there in a cool, dark corner of our consciousness. Society has taught us from the time we could understand language that happiness and men are one and the same. It is in our music, in our plays, in our books, on our TV screens, and in the center of 90 percent of the advertising that is thrown at us. We must buy this product, live in that type of home, and change our personality and body to match a certain type of woman in order to attract the right man. And it will be through him that happiness will come.

We have learned this since the time we were children. Every little girl knows that Barbie must have her Ken or there will be no prom night. There is no reason to wear the beautiful gown, no way for the admiring glances to come her way, no drifting away on a cloud of music if there is no Ken. He is the key to it all. From the story of Sleeping Beauty to the latest romance novel (even a Christian one), we are conditioned to believe that a man's love will be the answer to all of life's problems.

Not only are we conditioned by society to believe that having the right man will provide happiness, but we are even drawn by biology to seek these things through the male. Men are taller, stronger, and more aggressive than females. That in itself suggests security, and security must always be a prerequisite for happiness, we believe. We are built with sexual needs and a strong nesting instinct. These are most naturally filled by the faithful love of a good man.

Even certain aspects of our spiritual life and training can encourage us to seek our happiness and security from a man. As we discussed in chapter 1, God told Eve in Genesis 3:16 that her desire would be toward her husband. The picture of an ideal, godly home with a loving man in leadership is supported again and again throughout the Bible. Because of our fleshly minds, it is natural for us to take this godly, ideal model and blend it with the happy-ever-after fairy tale of Cinderella. We can easily get God's ultimate model and the worldly mold mixed.

As Christians, we are told not to let the world force us into its mold (Romans 12:2). But when the mold looks comfortable, secure, and desirable, and when it so closely resembles the ideal goal of God, we often baptize the mold and come up with a "Christian" version of the world's desires. We can be guilty of believing that if we had a truly godly husband as our mate, then all our problems would be solved and happiness would flow like a river. This is the old, unbiblical thinking wrapped in a pious bow. We begin looking to a man to provide us with what God said He alone could provide: Security. Happiness. Love. We may even be coming very close to the same sin the Romans committed when they exchanged the glory of God for the image of a man (Romans 1:23).

SHOULDN'T I HAVE ANY *SHOULD*S?

When I confronted Jenny about the many *should*s and *ought*s that she was applying to her husband, she bristled and immediately became defensive. "But you seem to think I shouldn't have any *should*s! What do you want me to do? Roll over and play dead? Don't I have a right to expect certain things from Ted? Doesn't God expect him to treat me right and supply my needs?" The answer to her question was both yes and no.

Yes, God does have a list of *should*s for husbands, and no, we should not keep our own private list. We don't need a list because God's list covers everything. His list is so extensive that even Prince Charming would have to struggle to measure up. According to God's *should* list, men should be good financial providers (1 Timothy 5:8); be such spiritual leaders that they are downright holy in all they do (1 Peter 1:15); be fair-handed and wise in child discipline (Ephesians 6:4); love their wives with an open, sacrificial, unconditional love (Ephesians 5:25); always possess self-control (1 Peter 1:13); and be full of gentleness, kindness, and humility (Colossians 3:12).

But before we pat ourselves on the back for not being half as strict on our husbands as the Lord is, we'd better read the rest of the Word because He has a list that applies to wives as well. Wives should be quiet and gentle in spirit (1 Peter 3:4); be filled with respect for their husbands (Ephesians 5:33); possess such righteous conduct as to be noted for holiness (Ephesians 1:4); and be willingly, wonderfully submissive (Ephesians 5:22-24).

A careful reader will notice that some of the above references apply to both husband and wife. They were not written to either sex alone, but to all Christians. God's list of *should*s for all of us is high. Very high.

When we let go of our brief and incomplete list of *should*s and allow God to set the standards for our husbands, a couple of curious things happen. First, because it is God's list and not ours, God is responsible for judgment when husbands fall short. It is God's job to mold the man to His standard; our job is to observe and encourage. We don't need to shape up our man or feel crushed when he will not conform to the standard.

Second, when we accept God's *should* list for others, we must also accept His list for ourselves. As a result, we see the need of giving both others and ourselves a lot of grace when either of us falls short of the goal. Jesus Christ paid the price for the difference between what we as wives and mothers are and what we ought to be. He also paid the price for the man who falls short. We grossly violate His grace when we try to extract a pound of flesh from the man to satisfy a debt that has already been marked Paid in Full.

TWO VIEWS OF WHAT MEN ARE

Growing up side by side with our ideals of what men should be is our idea of what men really are. This deeply held view is developed from experience and outside information, and, just like our *should*s, it colors all our opinions and relationships with men. This is our gut-level reaction to men in general. It is the assumption we make about their motives and the suspicion we have of how they will behave in the future. This picture is not the idolized man of our *shoulds* and *oughts*, but the real flesh and blood man. Like the ideal man, this man is formed over time, and often we are not even aware that he is coloring our outlook on life.

Our ideas of what real men are may sharply contrast with our idealized dream of what they should be. An example would be a woman who believes that men should possess great internal strength but who deep down believes that men are basically weak creatures who will never accomplish much.

Some women have very little bias in their views of what men are. For others, this bias is so strong that it makes it very difficult for them to live balanced, healthy lives. If, at the very base of experience, a woman believes that men are unreliable and want women for no other reason than to gratify their sexual lust and have an unpaid maid, she may have a very difficult time adjusting to the natural demands of marriage. No matter what her husband does or says, it will come to her through her preconceived ideas of what he "really" means and cause her pain.

I have chosen to describe two extreme views that women sometimes hold about men. I chose to use extremes because they are easier to identify than the gray, misty field called average. Your own ideas of what men are will probably fall somewhere between these two extremes, but seeing the continuum between them may make it easier to identify your own biases.

The first extreme is the woman who is firmly convinced that men are basically bad and are responsible for all the evil of the world. The other is that men are

always right, and if there is any problem, then somehow, someway it is bound to be a woman's fault.

MEN ARE RESPONSIBLE FOR EVERYTHING BAD THAT HAS EVER HAPPENED TO THE WORLD

In the mind of this woman, if the dollar falls on over-
seas markets or the lawn needs mowing or she breaks a
fingernail on the car door, there is bound to be a man
at fault somewhere! She can even give you reasons this
is logical. After all, since men control the political process, they are responsible for all wars and economic
problems, including the fall of the dollar. Because men
are supposed to be the leaders of the home, if any
chore is left undone, it is clearly their responsibility.
Even the broken fingernail was probably caused by a
door handle designed by some man!

We might expect these women to look like lady wres-
tlers and spend all their time marching for some radical cause, but that is not always the case. I have met a
couple of frail, little ol' ladies on church pews who
could manipulate facts with such sweet, longsuffering
smiles that it was only by the most careful listening one
heard how they were making men out to be the scourge
of the world. These women often come across as mar-
tyrs and victims. If a child goes wrong, it is the father's
fault for not giving him enough attention. If the car
breaks down, it is the fault of the male mechanic who
was out to take advantage of an innocent woman. If the
church splits, it is the fault of the men for failing to take
the lead. If she becomes a sour old maid by the age of
thirty-five, it is the man's fault for choosing a bubble-
headed blond for a wife instead of a quality woman like
her.

Of course, there are times when things are the fault

of a man (or even men in general), but when the source of every woe and every injustice and every failure is consistently the fault of a male, something is wrong with the woman's reasoning. By training and experience, she has learned to lay everything at the doorstep of man's responsibility. I think there is also an element of choice involved because using a man as a scapegoat becomes very convenient after a while. After all, things must be either his fault or her fault, and it is a lot more comfortable to believe they are always his!

I believe one reason some Christian women lean toward this extreme is that our heritage and teaching may have made it easy for them to do so. Could it be that we have put so much emphasis on male leadership in recent years that we have given women a convenient cop-out from all personal responsibility?

Many little girls grow up in church and never see or even hear an example of a strong, responsible, godly woman. In some denominations women are never asked to pray, and they never serve in any public capacity other than teaching small children and perhaps singing in the choir. Finding a modern role model can be difficult in these churches. I am not talking about women serving as pastors or taking over church leadership, but only being seen on occasion as responsible and capable Christians.

Not only do we have few modern role models, but also we often overlook biblical role models. How long has it been since you heard a good sermon that used a woman as a noble subject? Usually, the only way we think of Bible women is as they are related to some Bible man. They are someone's wife, someone's daughter, someone's mother, but seldom are they seen as persons in their own right. Even when they are discussed, it is often only in regard to something dumb they have done. We talk of

Eve tempting Adam with the forbidden fruit or of Sarah suggesting Abraham have a son by her handmaid. But we seldom hear of the noble sacrifice of Jephthah's daughter, of the fiery justice in the nature of Deborah as she led the nation to victory, of the courage of Miriam, of the intelligence of Priscilla. If girls never see a woman taking on real leadership in the church and never hear of an honorable woman in the Word, how will they learn to see themselves as responsible creatures?

We often don't see female strength and responsibility in our Bible study because we read the Word through the filter of our own culture and teaching. I read Luke 8:3 for fifteen years and clearly heard it say that a group of women followed Jesus from Galilee and "ministered unto him of their substance." Because of my culture and training, I assumed that the work these women were engaged in had to do with helping out with the laundry or stirring up an occasional pot of stew for the men. I was surprised when a little word study revealed that their "substance" was dollars and their "ministry" was to bankroll Jesus' traveling seminary!

When women are not given a proper balance of Bible teaching that accents female responsibility as well as submission, and when they have no examples of strong, able Bible women, it is easy for some to come to the angry conclusion that females are so helpless and worthless that God gave them a free ride in the baggage compartment of life. An attitude like that will make it easy for a woman to blame men en masse for everything from political corruption to hangnails.

NOTHING CAN EVER BE THE FAULT OF A MAN
At the other extreme is the woman who cannot tolerate the thought of men having any weakness, lack, or

blame. A test that makes it easy to spot women who lean to that end of the scale is to see how they react to news of a divorce between couples they hardly know.

I was amazed to overhear such a discussion between two acquaintances the other day. The first woman asked for prayer for a friend who was going through a divorce. The second woman, a godly prayer warrior, asked a few questions and was genuinely grieved over the trouble of this couple she did not know. But she also firmly stated that if the wife had only been more submissive, the tragedy would never have happened.

The first woman explained that she did not believe submission was the problem. The husband was having an affair, and the wife had caught him. Her prayer partner suggested that the affair was actually the wife's fault because she did not meet his sexual needs. The first woman rebutted that it was not the husband's first affair, but her prayer partner seemed deaf to the possibility that the husband might be at fault. Her thoughts still cycled to blame the wife—a woman she did not even know. If the wife had only been submissive enough, the woman insisted, the man would never have left her.

This strange phenomenon fascinates me every time I see it. Some women are compelled to whitewash only the men close around them, like a father or husband or son. For example, a woman says her father was not to blame for abandoning the family when she was five; it was her mother's fault or her own fault for driving him away. Her husband's torrid affair is not his fault; she is to blame for his sin because she is overweight. Her son's drug addiction is not his fault; a girlfriend made him do it.

Other women will expand their illogical defense of men to a wide variety of circumstances. Before my mother-in-law died, her favorite topic was "modern women" and how they had ruined the world. She perfomed amazing mental gymnastics to support some of her claims. She was firmly convinced that the campus unrest of the sixties was a direct political result of women getting the vote. "Everyone knows that women only vote for the one they think looks the best," she explained. But when I reminded her that she, too, voted on occasion, she said that was different because she always voted the way her husband told her to! To her mind, modern women were the cause of every ill of the nation.

I don't think too many women would go quite so far as to blame all political problems on women's voting power, but some do get very uncomfortable when logic and circumstances point the finger of guilt in the direction of a man, especially a man in authority. They only seem content when the trouble source can be traced to women in general or to themselves as part of the female race.

It may seem strange at first that a woman would want to view herself or the female sex as responsible for all problems, but there can be distinct advantages to this twisted logic.

For one thing, this pattern of reasoning may be a family pattern that is comfortable because it is familiar. If she grew up listening to Grandma take responsibility for Grandpa's bad temper and Mama take responsiblity for Daddy's inability to hold a job, she may find it natural to blame herself because her boss makes passes at her. The logic feels right to her even though it may seem totally illogical to everyone else. Continuing to follow the same family pattern she has always known has the advantage of not requiring the woman to grow or change.

Another advantage is that if we convince ourselves that it is our fault, then the power to change the situation still rests in our control. If a wife is sure that the reason her husband drinks is because she did not stop him or help him enough when he was helpless, then there is a distant hope that she can change the situation through personal determination. If she can take responsibility, then she has control. If she will reason with him enough, bail him out of jail one more time, shame and belittle him enough, be the perfect mother to him as well as the perfect wife, then surely she can change him. But if she places the responsibility squarely on his shoulders, then she also admits that the solution to the problem must come from him—and that is scary.

Seeing ourselves or women in general as always being at fault can be a security factor. If we view a man as being the source of our happiness and security, then the thought of his failure is a great and immediate threat to our welfare and to that of our children.

There are women who cannot stand to think of men being chosen by God for leadership and still possessing feet of clay. They need the men in their lives to be strong and without fault. If a man has a crack in his armor, one of these women will patch it by convincing herself that the crack is actually part of her and not really present in him at all. This maneuver keeps her safe.

THE POWER OF PERCEPTION

Judy Mamou in her book, *The Other Woman,* tells the story of her life as a stripper and how Jesus changed her. Part of that story involved her search for a new gimmick for her act. She wanted something that would make her strip stand out in the audience's mind, something that would make her special. That was difficult because, after all, one young woman stripped naked is not a whole lot different from another young woman stripped naked.

Then she had a new idea. She would incorporate snakes into her act! They would be part of her dance! At first she found the snakes repulsive, but in time they became her pets—and finally the only friends of this lonely, troubled woman.

Judy took excellent care of her snake friends. She would go to any lengths to make them comfortable and meet their needs. Each year when the snakes shed their skins, Judy would put a little water in her bathtub and lift the heavy reptiles into this new home so that the moist environment would make it easier for them to wriggle out of their tight and drying skins. She would spend hours seated beside the tub, rubbing her friends and making them comfortable.

One day during molting season, the Avon lady came to her door. After an hour of going over the catalog and sniffing the new fragrances, the sale was completed and the Avon lady asked to use the rest room before she left. Momentarily forgetting that she had been soaking her snakes, Judy graciously pointed the way. A few moments later, the Avon lady was heard screaming. She raced out of the bathroom, out of the house, and down the street running as fast as she could—which was not very fast because her panties were down around her knees!

It would be easy to jump to the conclusion that the bathtub full of snakes made the Avon lady run away with her pants down, but that is not really true. What had made the Avon lady run was how she perceived the snakes. She thought of them as awful, ugly, and danger-ous. Judy thought of them as friendly, gentle, and an asset to her career. The reason the snakes had such different effects on the two women was that each woman perceived the snakes in a completely different way. The perception made the difference.

We all have many perceptions that have formed throughout our lives. We have perceptions about ourselves, society, God, and many other things. We also have basic perceptions that we have formed concerning men. How they should behave. What they ought to think. What they really are inside. What we can expect of them.

The first step for any woman who wants to get out of the snow and into God's warmth and security is to examine what her perceptions are concerning men in general and the man she is married to in particular.

Some good questions to ask are: What *should*s and *ought*s make me angry when they are not carried out the way I think is correct? Where did I learn these? How quick am I to lay the responsibility for problems at a man's feet? How insistent am I on viewing myself and/or all females as holding the responsibility for (and the power over!) men?

This self-examination is not the entire answer, and it can be a little painful, but it is more comfortable than spending another year in the snow. In the end, it will be much easier to change your perceptions than it will to change either your circumstances or your man!

FOUR
WHO, ME?
WORK?

In 1975 I published my first book, *The Happy House-wife*. Four years later, I finished high school and received a GED certificate. In 1979 my second book came out, and my husband was killed. For the next six years I ran the cattle ranch he left me, and in 1985, when I was a grandmother past the age of forty, I entered college as a freshman.

My first book was the fulfillment of a lifetime of dreams. I had wanted to be a writer since early child-hood. When my dream at last became a reality, I assumed that life would be much easier than it had been. I was an author. My life would now be different. Organizations would be asking me to travel and speak. Other books would follow. Women would look up to me and write me letters asking for my advice. At last I could get busy full-time with the Lord's business and stop worrying about such mundane things as how to make the food budget stretch and where we would get the money for the children's school clothes.

But the Lord's plans were very different from mine, and what actually happened during the next few months was beyond my wildest dreams (or perhaps I should say nightmares).

The Happy Housewife was a success. It was reprinted in three languages and recorded for the blind, and it remained in print for five years. But at the same time as it came to print, the cattle market crashed. What profits the book brought in went to keep the bank from repossessing the family farm. Money problems were worse than ever, and it soon became obvious that if our family wanted to eat as well as pay the bank, someone would have to find a full-time job in addition to the normal ranch work.

I'll never forget that fateful morning when Bill sat at our kitchen table brooding over the newspaper want ads. He looked so defeated and alone. I was making coffee and doing what I thought good wives were supposed to do in situations like this: working hard to lift Bill's spirits. I gently reminded him how faithful God had been in the past and how nothing was beyond His control. I poured fresh coffee in his cup and gave him a warm, reassuring embrace. Then I asked if there were any prospects for work in the paper. "I don't see anything for me," he answered. "But here's one you could handle."

I couldn't believe my ears! Who, me? Work? How could he even think of sending the "Happy Housewife" out to punch a time clock? Mothers were not supposed to work outside the home, and I was a mother four times over. I had two children in grade school and a third just starting kindergarten, and the baby of the family was only three. How could I work? I already had a job.

But I had promised to help in this critical situation, and at that moment the kind of help we needed was the kind that could buy a pair of shoes! So, reluctantly, sadly, full of sighs and remorse, I answered the ad and started my route selling Avon products door to door. All the while my head was bowed and my shoulders slumped as I moaned, "Surely, Lord, this *can't* be Your will!"

When my husband sent me out into the work force, he sent out a bewildered, frightened, resentful, hurt woman. And more than that—an angry one. I was angry with him and angry with God. How could this happen? I had served God faithfully. I had been a loving and obedient wife. My children needed me. And besides all that, the outside world scared me to death!

The idea of being a working mother was totally foreign to everything I believed about marriage and Christian homes. Men were supposed to be the financial rocks of the family. It was Adam who had been charged with earning a living, not Eve! I was insulted at the idea of carrying my load as mother and part of his load as father, too.

Needless to say, my short-lived career as an Avon lady was stormy and unsuccessful. In fact, it almost ended in divorce.

IN RETROSPECT

It has been fifteen years since that early experience in the marketplace, and at various times I have worked as a secretary/bookkeeper, sold decorated birthday cakes from my home and insurance in an office, and been a writer, a general building contractor, a cattle rancher, and a caseworker for the Texas Welfare Department. The most enjoyable job I have held was doing part-time public relations work for a fairly large TV station, and the worst was working as a seamstress on a factory assembly line.

I consider myself fortunate that most of these jobs were only of short duration. I was able to be a full-time mother during most of my children's growing-up years. The longest I worked at any single job was the five years I ran the cattle ranch after Bill died. But every job had its own set of problems, and almost always my spiritual life went into a nosedive when I worked outside the home.

Looking back, I have wondered how it could have been made easier. Was there some magic key or some defense I could have used that might have kept life in better balance? Was there a perspective that could have made my lot less painful?

Yes. I believe it would have been easier if I had only been willing to take the same spiritual principles that I applied to other areas of my life and apply them to the complications of holding down a job.

LOOKING AT WORK THROUGH SPIRITUAL EYES

It was estimated in the 1980s that 52 percent of all American women were actively in the work force. Of this group, 59.1 percent were married women with children between the ages of six and seventeen, and 43.2 percent were married women with children under six years of age. Among divorced women in the labor force, 83.4 percent had children ages six to seventeen and 68.9 percent had children age six or younger. (Figures total more than 100 percent because some women had children in both age groups.)

Women who hold full-time jobs are often forced to try to be more than one person. They stretch themselves into pieces and find they are part breadwinner, part mother, part wife, and part woman in search of a personality. Psychologists have even coined a new term to express the problems of these women: role overload.

Frequently, women in the labor force find they are overworked and underpaid. This problem is bad enough for the unsaved woman, but I believe the Christian woman has even more struggles. Often her job directly conflicts with what she believes to be her duty as a mother and her expectations of a husband who will be a leader and provider. At the end of each weary day, these women are often uptight, stressed-out, stretched to the breaking point, angry, and guilt-ridden. That dismal portrait does not apply to all working women, but it surely applied to me.

It seems that every time I faced this trying situation, the Holy Spirit would bring certain questions to mind. When I was willing to answer these questions honestly, things were better. The situation might not change, but I would change on the inside, and that made all the difference. I would like to share them with you in the hope that if you face the same situation, you may answer them more quickly than I did and avoid some of the pain!

Why am I working?

It is amazing how much time we Americans spend acting and how little time we spend thinking! In our fragmented, get-it-done-yesterday life-styles, we simply don't have time to consider why things are going on. It is hard enough to grab the whirlwind of daily struggle by the tail and hang on for dear life! But if we are ever going to cope with the problem of punching a time clock, we have to examine why we are in the work force in the first place.

Why are we working? Why did we choose to leave our children for others to raise while we sold our skills on the open market? Could any motivation ever justify making a choice like that?

Many women drift into careers. They go to work when children are small to help pay off Christmas bills or a new refrigerator, and twenty years later they are still on the job. They have never slowed down long enough to consider whether there might be another alternative or what God's will might be in the matter.

I think these are the women who suffer most from guilt and anxiety. While chasing after the family "need" for a new Suburban van or backyard pool, they briefly wonder if they are doing the right thing. But they quickly bury those doubts and race off to work without an answer. Because they choose to make no decision about priorities, nothing they do feels quite right.

The truth is that no decision *is* a decision. When we refuse to set priorities about work, home, and family, we make immediate feelings and whims our top priority. This always bring trouble!

Other women deliberately choose to work and feel their choice is justified and blessed by God. These are not all career women searching for self-fulfillment or even women searching for the middle-class American life-style. Instead, they are daughters of the King who have weighed all the options and believe that working full- or part-time is the best way to be about their Father's business.

For example, I have known women who felt that Christian schools were so important for their children that they took a full- or part-time job in order to pay the tuition. The husband of a dear friend of mine surrendered his life to the ministry when her two children were in grade school. She took her first job to put him through seminary. After that, he pastored several churches that could not support a full-time pastor, so she worked that he might devote his complete attention to the ministry. When a woman has a willing attitude, ordered priorities, and the support—not *demand*—of her husband, she seldom suffers the complications that often accompany female employment.

Still other women feel they have no choice but to work. Illness, death, divorce, union strike, singleness, layoff, poor economy, inflation, poor financial planning, or any one of a dozen other crises have become part of their daily reality. They must work if they and their families are to have the basic food and shelter they need. If there was any choice involved in whether or not to work, life and its circumstances made it for them. When I looked at my own reasons for working outside the home, this is the category in which I most often found myself.

It might seem in many situations that the question of why we work is unimportant. Yet it has been my experience that at those times when a woman feels resentment or guilt in the pull between a job and the home, the question of why becomes more important than ever. Knowing why we took a job can make the difference between viewing ourselves as victims of circumstance or as victors in Christ.

The truth is, we do have a choice about going to work. No matter how bad our circumstances, we have a choice. We can choose to let our children go without food. We can leave the kids and run away with a trucker from Alabama. We can retreat back into ourselves until we became catatonic and are unable to walk or feed ourselves. We can choose to live in an institution and let our children become wards of the state. We can choose suicide.

Other mothers have selected from these options, and we could have, too. But we chose to work because we value ourselves and our kids so much that these other choices were unacceptable.

We demonstrated our priorities when we accepted our responsibility—no matter how unpleasant the responsibility—and chose what we believed to be the most honorable action under the circumstances: work.

Answering the question of why we are working is an all-important step in dealing with what can be a crisis situation.

How am I dealing with my anger?

Not all working mothers are walking ammunition factories waiting to explode, but most women who work will experience some degree of anger, especially if they do not really want to be in the labor force. We need to look for and admit to our anger toward God and our husbands before we can move past it and make a good adjustment to our new situation.

Many counselors estimate that 70 percent of their clientele are women. In that group, one of the most frequently encountered problems is depression. When we consider that the major cause of depression is unexpressed anger, we get some idea of the seriousness of this emotion.

Anger is such a sneaky emotion! It hides behind physical symptoms, such as ulcers or headaches, and masquerades by other names, like depression or stress. It is so slippery that one of the first problems with anger is to find it and paste a proper label on it.

Being a Christian can make it even harder to identify anger. We often swallow our emotions and cover up our distress because we want to handle things in a "Christian" manner. We think of anger as an unacceptable emotion—or even a sin—so we want to get rid of it the moment it peeks around a corner.

Another reason anger is so hard to identify is that it doesn't necessarily follow a logical pattern. We can know in our heads that it wasn't our husband's fault the union went on strike, but that doesn't keep us from being mad at him because it happened. We can even feel angry when one of our loved ones has a long-term illness or dies.

A working woman often experiences deep anger. Sometimes this anger is directed at her husband for not providing financially. Other times it can be directed at God for putting the family in a difficult position. It may be anger that is logically justified (e.g., "I wouldn't be in this position if that bum would pay his child support!"), or it may be totally illogical (e.g., "How inconsiderate of John to die and leave me with all these hospital bills!"). But whatever its source, the first step to healing is to admit our anger exists. That isn't always easy.

The first step in dealing with anger is a big one, but the second step is even more difficult. We have to move past our knowledge that anger is there and go on to accept the situation that made us angry in the first place. We must move past the pain into faith. We choose to believe that God is still in control and is working all things together for our good.

The good news about anger is that it is acceptable to God. He understands it. Anger is emotional energy, not a sin. It can lead us into sinful actions, but we are not sinning simply because anger exists. Ephesians 4:26 says, "Be ye angry, and sin not." In this verse we see that God almost commands us to be angry and admit to our emotion. The warning is that we not let our emotions lead us into sin.

Can I believe that God is good and is still in control?

This brings us to the toughest question of all. This

one question is the central issue of all Christian endeavor. This is the question that all Christians "grow" into.

I don't believe it can be answered once and never again. It has been my experience that I will firmly answer it in one situation. I'll say I have no doubt and my faith will be firm from that point until forever, only to find the same old question has to be answered all over again when I face a different circumstance a few years later. Can I trust in the goodness and power of God even when things look bad?

This is without a doubt the most difficult question I have ever faced in both my private life and my role as a counselor. If God is good, why does He allow so much pain? If He is good, why doesn't He change it? If He can't change it, why am I praying to Him?

It isn't always easy to see God's goodness in a difficult situation. We know God said He was working all things for our benefit, but evil and pain are real. How can God be good and in control and yet allow a mother to be forced to leave her weeping, frightened three-year-old with strangers at the day-care center because his daddy ran off with another woman and the rent will be paid this month only if she shows up at work on time?

It is one thing to answer this question when we sit comfortably on a church pew, but it is another thing entirely to answer it when we are faced with a situation we don't like. Sometimes this situation involves our work.

Each individual faces this question alone. Others may advise and witness; books may encourage and help. But in the final analysis, each Christian answers for himself, alone.

In moments of doubt, I am so grateful that God is not looking as much at my feelings as at my faith. Believing in His goodness and power is a choice I make with my will, not with an emotion. I choose to believe His Word. I decide that I will trust and accept as truth what He has said about His own goodness even when He leads me into a painful situation. That is hard, but the battle-field of faith never has been a place for cowards.

One Scripture that has become very dear to me in the past few weeks is Matthew 7:9-11:

> Which of you, if his son asks for bread, will give him a stone? Or if he asks for a fish, will give him a snake? If you, then, though you are evil, know how to give good gifts to your children, how much more will your Father in heaven give good gifts to those who ask him! (NIV)

I have been going through a particularly difficult trial recently. As I examine my situation, I find myself feeling as though God is passing out warm, fresh bread to all His other children. But when I hold out my hand, He drops a rock into it. That's what my feelings have told me.

But I know that another element is operating in my life—the element of faith. God has said He will never give me rocks for bread. I have a choice to believe my feelings or to believe His Word. When I repeatedly choose to believe His Word, my feelings get better. And in the end, I know I can quote Psalm 144, "Praise be to the Lord my Rock, who trains my hands for war, my fingers for battle" (NIV). It is the trying of our faith that brings patience, character, and hope (Romans 5:3-4).

Have I explored all other options?

The previous three questions might be called "big" questions. They are heavy and theological and require soul-searching. But there is one more question that I have to include—the question of options.

Too often our mind gets stuck in one pattern of thinking, and the Lord couldn't squeeze in a new idea if He greased it. Yet sometimes an inventive, new idea is just what is needed when it looks like going to work is the only way out of a family crisis. We usually think that working means we will spend eight hours away from home doing something that someone else tells us to do. But there are other possibilities, and it is always good to explore a few.

Some Christian psychologists advise that mothers be away from their children no more than one hour per day for each year of the child's age. A baby who is one year old can have its mother leave for an hour each day on a regular basis without either the baby or the mother showing signs of undue stress. A child of four seems to do well without its mother for a maximum of four hours each day. It is interesting to note that we send our children to school when they are six and most school days are six hours long.

This principle of an hour per day per year of life is the ideal maximum. It does not, of course, include special occasions—such as when the mother of a two-year-old leaves junior with grandmother while she spends all afternoon Christmas shopping—and it does not mean that a mother *should* be away from her child every day. But for mothers with a choice, it is good to plan on being gone consistently no more than one hour per year of life. Some counselors feel that mothers who spend more time away from their children run a greater risk of future problems and poor adjustment in the kids.

It is facts like these that haunt women who must work in order to live. They sometimes end up feeling as though God is squeezing the toothpaste tube at both ends. On the one hand, He gives them children to raise, and on the other hand, He puts them in a situation where the only honorable choice they can make is to take full-time employment!

At this time, ingenuity and inspired ideas are most needed, and the good news is that all these ideas don't have to be personally generated. Magazine articles, the public library, friends, and Christian bookstores can all be sources for ideas of ways to earn money while staying at home all or most of the time.

Cottage industry seems to be enjoying a new strength. These days women, or even whole families, produce and sell everything from potted plants and custom clothing to vegetarian sandwiches that are sold to health-conscious office workers. I believe that as the trend for women in the workplace continues, an even greater demand will be created by the vacuum they leave at home. Demands for child care, food catering, house cleaning, yard work, grocery shopping, school tutors, and someone to pick up and deliver kids from point A to point B can all be turned into money.

I read, for example, of two neighbors who both needed jobs. They got a loan from the bank and turned the garage of one home into a Christian day-care center. This job not only let them raise their own children, but also allowed them to be a witness to others. And it generated all necessary income for both families.

Computers, fax machines, and phone lines linked to offices have opened the windows for many women to spend less time at the office or in a long, useless commute.

However, one word of warning: Working at home is not magic and requires more dedication and self-discipline than punching a time clock. It is not for everyone, and it frequently requires the working mom to hire babysitters to come and take care of the kids while she gives full attention to the business.

Industry is beginning to recognize the value of providing jobs that take a woman's motherhood into consideration. Part-time jobs are often available, and time-share jobs, where one person works four or five hours in the morning and someone else works the same desk in the afternoon, are more common than ever. Other employers are providing child care facilities on the job site.

If you are stuck in a dead-end, low-pay, eight-to-five routine that you hate and you feel you need to be home, put your head and heart and prayer and Christian principles into a search for something else. The solution may not come next week or even next year, but keep on praying and thinking. In time the Lord may show a way of making money that is tailor-made for your particular situation.

THE WORKING WOMAN?

Sometimes I hear Christians speak with wistful longing about a past, simpler time when the only thing mothers had to do was to be good mothers. They believe that in such a distant time, women never worked, and every Christian man was a leader and provider in his home. These women may comment that they were born in the wrong generation and say they would have been much more content in a "Little House on the Prairie" life-style. But somehow I doubt that. Life may have been slower at one time, but it has never been simpler, and women have always worked.

In 1960 I married the baby of a family of nine. My husband's mother had grandchildren older than me.

They were rural East Texas farmers; I was a sixteen-year-old teenybopper fresh out of southern California. To say there was a generation gap between myself and my mother-in-law was an understatement. My mother-in-law had at one time moved from Texas to Oklahoma in a covered wagon. I wore short shorts and red lipstick and danced to Elvis records.

Mrs. Baker saw a lot of changes in her life and did a better-than-average job of adjusting. I will always be grateful for the effort she exerted in adjusting to me! However, one thing Mom Baker never could quite adjust to was those shameful, modern women who worked outside the home. She prided herself on the fact that she had never "worked." But as I listened to her tell stories of her life, that statement became increasingly hard to understand. It seemed to me that if anyone ever qualified as a working woman, it was Mom Baker.

Mom Baker did all of the things that women of her generation were expected to do. She milked the cows, churned butter, and sold it to the store in town. She sold her eggs, too. She raised the children, tended the garden, and cooked three square meals a day. None of that, of course, qualified as "work" because she was always within fifty feet of the house.

However, when times were tough, she was often forced to do routine jobs more distant from the house. Early in her marriage the house burned while she was down at the creek doing the washing and the older girls had been left to watch the younger children and finish cooking off the apple butter. No one was hurt in the fire, but they lost everything the family owned. Still, what Mom was doing at the creek was not considered being away at work, and the older girls were not thought of as baby-sitters.

When the factory opened up in town, her family was still struggling with the effects of the Depression, so her husband took a job doing shift work there. Mom plowed the fields with her youngest baby in a fruit crate tied with a rope to the tractor fender. When the cotton crop came in, she kept the books, hired and fired the hands, made payroll at the end of the day, and cooked a noon meal to serve her own family plus thirty-five or more hired hands. Of course, that did not make her a member of that newly emerging group called "working women"!

When they began dairy farming, Mom had to be on the job at 4:30 A.M., so the children were left to get up, fix breakfast, and get to the school bus on their own. But none of this activity was considered "work."

When Mom was in her sixties, the neighbor who owned the ranch that connected with their east fence sold his property. The new owner converted it from a cattle ranch to a peach farm. He needed someone to sell his peaches during season and thought Mom would be the perfect choice. The peach shed was located less than one mile from her front door. The hours were flexible, the pay reasonable. The work was seasonal, and Mom wanted the job.

But working for pay outside the home went against every fiber of her moral being, and Dad was dead set against the idea. He said no wife of his had ever worked or ever would work because he was head of the house and could make it just fine without her help. Things were really tense for a while as Mom struggled with her own conscience and with Dad's stubbornness.

Finally, Dad said that he objected but would leave the final decision up to Mom. For the first time in her life, she crossed his will and took the job. Mom loved the job and worked for several seasons, but I always got the impression that she was a little embarrassed. She had finally done what she so often criticized others for doing. She had become a "working" wife.

FIVE
SAMSON,
WHERE ARE YOU?

When West Point went coed, the instructors who handled physical development and testing had a problem. The school had spent a hundred or so years developing an exercise and fitness program for men, but what would it do with the body of a woman? Should she be given a specially designed program that was easier than that of the male? Could you make a woman's body as strong as a man's body if you trained them both the same way?

After a lot of head scratching and debate, it was decided that the women who entered the military academy would get no special privileges and no special physical program. If they wanted the same credentials as men, they would meet the same requirements as men.

At the end of the semester, the cadets were all tested and ranked from the weakest to the strongest in the class. The exact same test was used for both male and female. When the results were in, the strongest person in class turned out to be a male. In fact, the top 98 percent were all male. Not one female name showed up on the list until the bottom 2 percent.

The military had tried to shape up these women. They had fed them the same as men, exercised them the same as men, placed the same demands on them as the men. But no matter what they did, the female body would not—could not—respond with the same strength as a man's.

When God created people, He made them male and female, not copy number one and copy number two. The sexes are different. In His wisdom, God ordained that men got the muscle and women got the fat. (Pound for pound, the female body contains more fat cells then the male.)

Now, I don't want to argue with God's arrangement, but when a woman is without a man, it seems to me that God is responsible to help her come up with some ingenious methods of making up for all of man's lovely, missing muscles. Lighting the pilot on a water heater, changing the spark plugs in a 1979 Chevy, patching a leaky roof, and opening a stubborn pickle jar are just a few of the skills they don't teach in Girl Scouts. These things are supposed to be "men's work," and we of the pampered sex are not expected to worry our pretty little heads about such things. But when no one is around—or the one who is around can't or refuses to exert his God-given talent—the practical aspects of daily living can become quite a problem for the woman who never thought she would have to struggle with such things.

She may be a fifty-five-year-old widow who can't get the lawn mower started or a pastor's wife whose husband can never find time to fix the cracked wall or a young mother struggling to put a bicycle together on Christmas Eve because her husband is away in the Navy. She may be a sixty-year-old spinster who can't move the sofa in order to retrieve her glasses that fell behind it, or a businesswoman whose husband can't help her carry in the groceries during a rainstorm because he is confined to a wheelchair. Or she may be a wife with kids and a full-time job whose husband will not mow the lawn on the weekend because he has to run off and play with a friend's new bass boat. But whoever she is, she can begin to think that God wasted muscles when He gave them to the male of our species.

A woman in situations like these has several choices. One, she can get mad at God because of the circumstances she has been handed. Two, she can get mad at the man because he won't take time to do the job. Or three, she can resent both God and the man because her husband can't do the job.

There is a fourth choice, but this one takes time. It is not the natural thing to do. It often can only be accomplished after the anger has been acknowledged and thoroughly felt. The fourth choice will not change her circumstances, and it will not change her man. Worse yet, it will probably have to be repeated over and over again before it will change the woman's feelings. But, all things considered, the fourth choice holds more hope than any of the others. In the end, it is the only choice that eventually brings peace.

The fourth choice is to give up trying to change the circumstances or the man and instead pour our efforts into changing our reaction. We can't always choose our situation, but we can always choose how we react to our situation.

FEEL THE ANGER BUT REACT IN FAITH

I pray that I am not misunderstood with this statement, but there are times when getting angry with God is the proper and healthful thing to do. Or, perhaps more accurately, there are times when admitting we are angry with God is the right thing to do. We don't always have total control over our feelings of anger, but we always have control over whether or not we admit those feelings. We also have control over what we let those feelings make us do.

For example, Mary may have prayed fervently that John would not leave her. She and the children needed him desperately. But when John does leave, and two weeks later the car breaks down, Mary can find herself feeling angry at God for allowing both incidents. When these feelings of anger surface, Mary can either admit she is angry with God, or she can deny the anger and emotionally swallow it.

It is OK to feel anger toward God and to tell Him so. He is a very big God. He created the universe with His Word. He is strong enough not to crawl off in a corner and pout or throw a temper tantrum and spit lightening bolts because one woman got upset with Him. It is much safer to respectfully express our emotions to the Lord than it is to swallow them and give ourselves ulcers.

Mary needs to live in truth and admit several things to herself. Yes, she is hurt. Yes, circumstances seem to indicate that God is not listening to her prayer. Yes, she feels angry, even angry at God.

But Mary dare not stop there. She needs to go on and move in faith and encourage herself in more of the truth that God has given. She needs to agree with God's Word when He carefully explains that He will never leave her or forsake her (Isaiah 49:15-16; Romans 8:31-39; Isaiah 43:2); that He really does have her best interest at heart (Philippians 1:6; Jeremiah 17:7-8; Luke 12:32), that no matter what the present circumstances, He is still in control and will provide a way through it

(Matthew 6:25-34; Proverbs 3:5-6; Isaiah 30:21). Also, by reading about the lives of Bible characters and listening to the testimony of other Christians, she needs to really grab hold of the fact that God does not settle all of His accounts at five o'clock each Friday. Complete justice will not occur until He personally comes back to the planet to take control.

There are some practical techniques that Mary could use to help her move through the expression of her anger and on to faith. I often encourage clients to write God a letter and tell Him how they feel. They don't need to accuse Him unjustly or call the Almighty names, but they simply need to tell Him what they are feeling. If they feel abandoned by Him, they need to say that. If they are feeling angry or confused or frightened, then they should use those words in the letter. It is a good idea to go into detail and tell God why the feelings are there, or if that is impossible, tell Him they can't understand the feelings and don't know where they come from. The main thing is just that they are honest and lay it out before Him just as it really is.

Once the feelings are out in the open, it is time for the next step to be taken—the step of faith. Often it will help if a person will *do* something to demonstrate his faith.

One thing that can be done is confession with the voice. A woman can take one of the above-listed Scripture references and speak it out loud, telling herself, the devil, and the Lord that she chooses to believe the words are true. If she feels too embarrassed or foolish to do this where she might be overheard by a family member, she can always go into the bathroom, close the door, look in the mirror, and speak softly to herself. For most of us, speaking the Word once out loud is ten times as effective as thinking it in our minds.

It can also be effective for a woman to take a sentence or a phrase from the Bible and write it on a card that she carries with her at all times. The card can fit in a pocket or a purse and be there as a reminder all through the day. Every time she reaches for keys or change, the feel of the card will remind a woman of God's assurance of care even if she doesn't have time to take the card out and read it.

One word of warning: As strange as it may seem, we can occasionally try *too* hard to use the Bible to fix a problem. It is possible to bite off the Word in large, undigestible chunks that really don't taste very good and force ourselves to swallow them by an act of self-discipline.

Sometimes people determine they will read three chapters a night. They open the Bible and begin at most any place the mood happens to strike. They work without system or much thought to the process, and it does them limited good. I would far rather see a client take one verse or even a part of a verse and deal with it over a week or a month, than to cover forty chapters and not understand or be able to apply a thing that she read.

Personally, I have one verse that I have been studying for a full year—John 15:16. It is not the only verse in the Bible I have read this year! I usually spend quite a few hours each week in Bible study, but this is the one verse that I carry with me and that is becoming part of me. If a Christian has one verse that is understood, memorized, and applied, it is worth more than many chapters read but not digested.

Another technique for moving in faith is to keep a journal. I sometimes think my mind leaks faster than my colander. The Lord may answer a half dozen prayers for me before I wake up and say thank you because I forgot what I prayed for as soon as I got my knees unbent. A notebook in which we regularly record our feelings and prayer requests will go a long way in aiding our slippery minds. All through the Word, God repeatedly tells His people to remember what He has done. He doesn't forget; we do. Few things can be better tools for building faith than a well-kept journal. How can we expect our heart to trust God with a future we can't see and don't know until we have practiced trusting Him with a past that we do know?

Another vital step in moving to faith is practicing forgiveness.

FORGIVENESS IS A CHOICE

We sometimes treat forgiveness as though it were the company china. It is something to be brought out only on rare occasions and used with care.

But forgiveness doesn't work that way. It comes closer to being like an exercise video. Using it once a year is likely to yield poor results. That is where any woman who can identify with standing in the snow has the advantage. She will have *lots* of opportunities to practice her forgiveness skills!

One place that opportunities will crop up weekly—if not daily—will be in the area of chores. Something will need to be done, but our man is gone or he is in the house but simply refuses to do the job. Maybe he is too occupied with other things. Maybe he doesn't see the problem as a real need. Maybe he is just stubborn and selfish. But whatever the cause, the fact remains that there is some kind of "man's work" that, in the woman's opinion, needs to be done—and her man is not cooperating!

These are the times when we need to take forgiveness out of our theological closets and dust it off for practical use. We don't have to wait for a big event to practice forgiveness. In fact, if we wait for the biggie to come along, we will probably fail because we did not exercise our spiritual muscles on smaller lessons.

Forgiveness only takes place in the presence of pain. Big pain or little pain, it doesn't matter. One must be hurt and admit to that hurt before forgiveness is possible. Experiencing hurt and then participating in forgiveness may be the most liberating and health-producing experience known to mankind. But before we discuss what forgiveness is, maybe we should make it clear what forgiveness is not.

Forgiveness is not stupidity. If Karen's ex-husband borrows money from her three times and never pays it back, she should forgive him three times. But that doesn't mean she has to loan him money again! It is a sin to borrow and not repay (Psalm 37:21). We are told that we must not share in the sins of others (1 Timothy 5:22), and if Karen loans this guy money again, she is simply making it easier for him to sin again. Karen can forgive her ex-husband completely and still keep a tight lock on her wallet.

Forgiveness is not dishonesty. We don't have to pretend that we are not hurt or deny the existence of pain in order to forgive. It is not forgiveness to paste a smile over clenched teeth and wave our hand and glibly say, "It doesn't really matter."

Forgiveness is not a feeling. Good feelings may come with forgiveness, but they are not necessary to its existence. In fact, the only feeling that must be connected with forgiveness is pain. If forgiveness were a good feeling, God would have been unjust when He commanded that we forgive others (Matthew 6:14). We have only limited control over our feelings, but we have every control over our decisions and actions.

Forgiveness is a decision. Forgiveness can exist without good feelings, but it can never exist without choice. When we choose by an act of our will to accept the hurt as part of our life and let the offender go free, then, and only then, has forgiveness taken place. We must turn the offender loose from our condemnation, free from our revenge, and free from any effort on our part to restore our lost rights. That is forgiveness.

Forgiveness can be used in the most common adversities. For example, our car gives out when we are thirty miles from home and we have two crying, hungry toddlers in the back seat. We *know* it would not have happened if the man we depended on had simply fixed the problem when we complained to him about it three months ago.

PRACTICAL SOLUTIONS

Let's go back to the illustration of the young woman with both a job and kids and a husband who runs off to play instead of mowing the lawn. She can choose to feel the anger but walk in faith and believe that God is aware of her situation and will provide a solution. She can take the big step of forgiveness, and even though the emotions may be boiling, she can choose to let go of her right for revenge. But that still leaves her with a lawn that looks like a jungle and an unfair portion of the work load on her back. What then?

It seems to me that her first step is to figure out how much emotional and physical and financial expense she believes the problem is worth. How important is it that the lawn be mowed that day? Oh yes, it is an irritation, and the neighbors may be talking behind closed doors, and surely if her husband would just get his act together the world would be a much more pleasant place.

But how much is she personally willing to pay to get that irritation out of the way? She does not have the option of making her husband spend his resources on it. He has already made his choice. She can probably make his life miserable when he does come home, but that still will not get the lawn mowed. How important is the lawn to her—not him? What will she give to get the job done?

If this young wife decides that the job is important to her, one solution she might choose is to pay someone else to do the job. That may sound radical if the young wife is on a tight budget. But, all things considered, it might be the better of the evils. If the lawn is important to her and she is embarrassed and stressed when it isn't done; if she can't change her husband and nagging him is forbidden by Scripture; if doing it herself creates tears of self-pity and resentment that build and last for days, then paying someone to cut it may be cheaper in the long run than a divorce or a hospital stay for stress-related disease.

There are many small jobs that a neighborhood teen may be willing to do for a few dollars. A woman alone who needs heavy boxes brought down from the attic, an older widow who wants a flower bed shoveled, or a divorcée who wants a tree house built for her son could each find possible sources of help through the church youth group. It may prove to be a two-way ministry as the woman gets the job done and the youth earn some needed money.

But it is sometimes very difficult to let go of money and pay someone to do a job we feel our husband had an obligation to do for free. Why should we pinch pennies and deny ourselves, then pay someone to do his job? One good reason is that it keeps us from two sins that are very easy to fall into: self-pity and revenge.

Joyce had a full-time job and three children. She also had a firm belief that men were responsible to maintain the family car. Her dad and brothers had always kept the old, black Ford looking like new. They spent each Saturday morning washing it and making sure the motor was in good condition. She was sure that even the Bible would support the philosophy that men should keep the cars in shape and women should clean the house. During the first few years of their marriage, her husband, John, seemed to agree also. Of course, that was before he learned how to play golf.

Five years into the marriage, Joyce was doing the house and the car. Every couple of weeks she would get angry and nag John. He would promise to get the job done, then someone would call to get up a foursome and he would be off to the course. Joyce would stay behind and fume. Angry and sullen, she would scrub the car herself. Every brush stroke became a statement of her self-pity and a reminder of his abuse. She was determined to do a better job on the car than John ever did, then she would park it in front of the house hoping he would feel guilty when he came home. He never did.

She talked to her mother about how John never helped her; she told the women's circle what a selfish man he was; she made sure the children knew how unfairly their dad was treating her, and she tried her best to stir up guilt in John—a manipulation he strongly resisted. Paying someone else to wash the car each week would have been an expensive strain on their tight budget, but the emotional price the family continually paid year after year was much higher.

LEARNING TO DO IT MY WAY

Of course, doing the job yourself is not always a bad option. If the man won't do it or can't do it, and the woman can yield herself to tackle the job with a decent attitude, the results can be very rewarding. She may surprise herself and find a talent she never knew she had.

When my husband, Bill, was killed by a drunk driver, I was thirty-five years old. I was a high school dropout and had just earned my GED two years earlier. We were ranchers with a cow/calf operation in East Texas and a custom hay-baling business. We had four children—two girls, ages eight and eighteen, and two boys, ages eleven and thirteen.

Although I had helped Bill on the ranch, running it myself was another story altogether, but I am proud to say that I did it. For five years I was the only cattle rancher I knew who wore nail polish under leather gloves. I was past forty before I sold the ranch, entered college as a freshman, and eventually became a counselor.

Being human is not easy. Living under normal conditions is challenging enough. But when circumstances beyond our control force us women to take on jobs that we thought the man of the house would always handle, something happens to the mental image we have of ourselves.

I always pictured myself dressed in pink lace serving plum pudding from a silver dish. When Bill died, I suddenly found myself under the car trying to figure out why the rebellious machine refused to function. The shock of reality was disconcerting. Sometimes I would shake my head in amazement and wonder if such absurd things ever happened to the ultrafeminine "total woman."

At discouraging moments when I was tempted to check my birth certificate to make sure it still said "female," I found it helpful to remember that men were not born with a wrench in their hand. They did not arrive on the planet knowing how to turn a screw or hammer a straight nail. They have ten fingers, two eyes, and one brain just like women. They, too, had to learn everything they know.

The first winter I was alone, the oil pump went out on my tractor. I cried and soaked in self-pity for an hour. Then—still protesting that I could never do it—I got out the owner's manual Bill had used so often and replaced all the rings and seals. I had never tackled anything more complicated than a sewing machine, but the tractor was still running efficiently when I sold it several years later.

It was also a great comfort to find that my questions were not as dumb as I thought they were. I had always assumed men knew what they were doing. They don't. I began to listen when I was in a hardware store or lumberyard or garage. Men say such things as, "You know that little gadget that fits on the thingamajig?" and "I don't know what's the matter with the car. It just sort of makes a *g-e-e-r-pop* sound when I turn the key."

Sometimes men don't know the technical names for items and need instructions from clerks and professionals. That knowledge made it much easier for me to insist that others explain things to me, especially if they were taking my money. Without embarrassment, I found I could force bankers, clerks, lawyers, doctors, and mechanics to take time to clearly tell me what was going on and why. If they refused to do so or acted insulted, there was another, more polite professional who would be glad to have my business. Asking questions and insisting on clear answers is not a sign of a weak feminine mind. It is good business practice.

But there are times when all that has been said thus far in this chapter is simply not enough. There are times when you can admit to the anger and move through it to faith and forgiveness, try all the practical solutions you can think of, struggle and make every effort to get the job done on your own, but still be faced with a situation where pure manpower is the only solution. What then? What do you do when you have read the instructions and asked the questions and tried your best and you still can't build it or fix it or move it? What about the times when you feel very feminine and defenseless and alone and you long for someone (preferably a husband) to take over the responsibility and get the job done?

THE HUSBAND WHO NEVER FAILS

I faced a problem like that in the spring of 1983 when I tried to build fences on part of the ranch. I had no real choice about building those three miles of fence. It had to be done if I was to continue to operate, but getting the project accomplished looked hopeless when I considered it logically. I could not afford to hire a man to help me. I had no previous experience building fence, even though I had helped Bill patch line. My sons were preteens and in school much of the time, so their help was minimal. Yet with courage and determination that still amazes me, we set out to do the impossible.

With hope and good, clean sweat, we built almost two miles of fence on level ground. It was stout, strong, and well built. I was proud of our accomplishment. But when we tackled the last mile of the fence along the road, my macho image began to fade, and the absolute impossibility of the task became evident.

To the east a fence already existed, but it had severe problems. This was a half-mile stretch of a fairly good fence that Bill had constructed new a few years before he died. As soon as he finished, I remember he said, "I really ought to go back and poison those tree and vine roots." He said the same thing every spring after that, but by the time I became responsible for that stretch of wire, slender elms and sweet gums had woven their way in and out of the wires and reached twenty-five feet high. In places the trees had grown completely around the wire, encasing the barbs in their wooden hearts. Wild roses and honeysuckle twisted among the wire, posts, and branches. It made a lovely sight in the spring, but the weight of the vines and the pressure of the growing trees had already damaged and would soon destroy the fence if something was not done. Making matters worse, an electric line tickled the top branches of the trees in this section.

The stretch to the west was still more hopeless. What passed for a fence was only a twenty-foot-thick strip of tangled underbrush, old trees three feet across the trunk, and bramble vines with one-inch thorns. All of this had been haphazardly pieced together with rusty wire by some ancient owner who made a "fence" by nailing the wire from tree to tree. The ground was rock-hard gravel. It went uphill and was laced with gullies. Worse yet, the fence would have to cross two creeks noted locally for the large, poisonous snakes that filled them.

I had put in many long, hard hours holding things together since Bill died, but this time the task was beyond me. Late one evening, after another fruitless day of effort without success, the boys walked to the house, leaving me alone in the meadow. Laying down my bruised pride, I had to admit that I was beaten.

I sat on the tailgate of the pickup wiping wood chips from my chain saw and watching the branches of the trees along the creek turn black against a pink and yellow sunset. I could feel wet tears making clean rivers down my dirty cheeks. It would take a crew of six men with large saws and a bulldozer to do the work that needed to be done, and I was only one woman with bruised legs, sore arms, and the help of two young boys. What do you do when things are impossible? Where do you go when you have tried your best and your best is not good enough?

"Lord," I prayed with a sigh, "You said in Your Word that You are a father to the fatherless. So, if You and I share the same kids, You must be my husband. And Husband, I wish You would get out there and do Your share of the work 'cause I am flat wore out!"

As soon as the words were out of my mouth, I felt ashamed. How presumptuous of me to talk that way to God! How foolish to order the Almighty! I apologized to Him immediately.

I spent the next day surveying the problem and trying to think of a new solution. If I could not remove the trees and build the fence right, what other choices did I have? If I built in front of the trees, would I not be dangerously close to the road? I called the road commissioner to ask him what the law said about roads and fences and trees.

The commissioner came to the ranch himself. He tramped up and down the hill and grunted. He poked under the bridge and grunted some more. Then at last he rubbed his chin and spoke. "We can't help you on the east fence, but . . ."

"Help?" I questioned. "The county might be willing to *help* me do the work?"

He ignored my interruption and restated his sentence. "We can't help with the east fence, but the law allows us to go a maximum of twenty feet into private property to clear right-of-ways, and this section of road is long past due a clearing. If you will only remove the old wire, we will come in with bulldozers and a crew of men. We'll level the land, shape a drainage ditch and pile the timber for you to burn. All you will need to do is build a new fence."

I was surprised right out of my boots! How wonderfully the Lord had provided! I sang His praise for two days while I snipped rusty wire and pulled it from the underbrush. The third day, I dressed in business clothes and drove into town to take care of some banking and do the marketing.

When I returned home, the children met me at the door claiming a man from the electric company had asked if he could clear the east fence. "I don't believe it," I stated flatly. "The electric company only cuts off the tops of the trees that threaten their wires. They do not clear fences. You kids must have heard the man wrong." But they insisted and told me to go ask the man for myself. "He is clearing the fence on the Johnson place now," they said.

Still in unbelief, I immediately drove up the hill and called what appeared to be the foreman away from his work. "Yes, ma'am," he explained. "The company is building a larger line through this area. We have been asked to cut all trees off at ground level unless the owner objects. Since your trees are in the fence, and we can't damage private property, we will have to clear the fence in order to remove the trees. If you will give your permission, I'll bring in a crew of men with chain saws and get started next week."

"Praise the Lord!" I said out loud, and in a few brief sentences told the puzzled young man how I was alone in the world and the Lord had sent him to take care of my problem. He was polite but unimpressed, and I knew my gentle Lord would not want me to push the subject. But as I turned to go, he asked, "By the way, ma'am, do you have a fireplace? We are also authorized to cut the trees into any size logs you desire." He looked at my high-heeled shoes and small hands, then suggested, "That is, if you could maybe hire some man to pick up the logs for you and carry them to your yard?"

It was so good to know I did have a Husband who was willing to help carry the load—a wise and caring heavenly Husband who would never fail.

SIX

THE ICY STREAM
OF LONELINESS

Every woman who has spent time standing in the snow
understands the meaning of loneliness. This loneliness
chills like a deep, cold river.

This cold river is not a single stream but many
branches and tributaries that all contribute to a single
icy flow. There is sexual loneliness, spiritual loneliness,
companionship loneliness, intellectual loneliness, and
social loneliness. Loneliness touches everyone occasionally, but for the woman in the snow, it can become
her only companion.

I can sympathize with the woman caught in that
chilling situation because it seems like I spent at least a
hundred years there myself. I remember three years
that were particularly difficult as I faced life from the
isolated vantage point of a farmhouse on the Oklahoma prairie.

Back in the early 1970s my husband, Bill, was in the
United States Air Force. He was part of the security
police force and worked shift work at the base. But he
hated living in base housing, so we had ended up in a
tiny frame house twenty-eight miles away from the base.

It was lonely out there with nothing but the wind and the grass, but Bill thought it was heaven. He went to the base each day and struggled with all the duties and pressures of his job, then came home to have his supper and rest.

We had one car between us, so the only time I left the tiny house was once each month to buy groceries at the commissary and once each week to take the children to church. Clothes and other supplies were either homemade or bought through catalog mail order. As a family, we left the house once a year each spring when we spent a week working cattle on my in-laws' ranch.

I spent three years in that small, two-bedroom house with no one but my three tiny children for company. We never ate out; we never went to a movie; we never had friends over; we never went to someone's house for coffee and games; we never went to a church social. However, I do remember attending one PTA meeting.

During those lonely years I was quick to blame my emptiness on my husband. "After all," I reasoned, "he is the one who wanted to live in the country, and he is the one who refused to take part in the social activities of the church."

In the years that followed, Bill continued to be a convenient scapegoat for my restlessness and feelings of isolation. No matter which tributary of the icy river was giving me trouble at a particular moment, be it social, mental, physical, or spiritual, I could find some reason he was to blame. If I was lonely, it was bound to be his fault. I was convinced that if he did not take the initiative to fix my loneliness, I was doomed to endure it. After all, I could not be expected to do anything about the situation!

A lot of time has gone by, and, I hope, a lot of maturing has taken place in my soul since those days on the prairie. I now see that Bill's refusal to join me in the things I thought socially important was only part of the problem. The second half of the problem was deep inside myself. Although I hate to admit to it, some of the problem was caused by my personal pride, laziness, and self-pity.

MEN DO PLAY A PART

I don't mean to suggest that men in general and husbands in particular are not to blame for a large part of the loneliness women feel. Men often create loneliness for a woman when they fail to meet their responsibilities as leaders. Sometimes they withdraw into their own world and leave her emotionally alone. Sometimes they leave her physically alone and take off with another woman. Some men don't know how to provide the intimacy a woman needs and others just don't care. Men have a great deal of power to help create loneliness in the lives of their wives.

First, they have the power because God gave them the leadership role in the family. When men refuse to adequately fill that role, an empty space is left in the heart of their wives. Ice forms in a place where some of the best flowers of marital intimacy should be growing.

Second, men contribute to a woman's loneliness simply because they *are* men. In our culture, men are a necessary link between women and the social world. They have automatically been granted a power of social standing just by being born male. Most brides still take the groom's name as their own. Most children are legally called by Daddy's last name, not Mama's. Telephone books usually list the family number by the man's name. The mailing address on junk mail and wedding invitations alike will often be a "Mr." and his name while the wife will only get a "Mrs." sandwiched in the middle. Cigarette advertisements may claim, "You've come a long way, Baby," but in our culture the social identity of the family is still represented through the man of the house. It is his name and his reputation that defines what the family is and what position it holds in the community.

Men are important to a woman's social standing in general, but I believe they are even more important to her church society. I suspect that few people realize how difficult it can be for a woman who finds herself alone after years of marriage or a woman whose husband does not attend church to feel at home in an organization that seems designed only for intact family units.

Many years ago before Bill died, I was a member of a small church. Our adult Sunday school class was warm enough and the teacher made a real effort to make everyone welcome. A few women who sometimes came to class were in the same position as I was in. Their husbands seldom or never came to church, and we spiritually single ladies never came to the socials.

I remember standing on the sidewalk one morning after church and talking with another woman who occasionally came to Sunday school about the possibility of joining the others for a night of snacks and dominoes. We knew there would be about fifteen sets of husbands and wives present, and we would be the only singles. Everyone would be bound up two by two and all the tables set for four. Janet thought for a moment and then told me she might come, she wasn't sure. At first I thought I might risk going alone, but the thought of being odd man out at a table was just too much. I stayed home.

Now I am on staff with a very large metropolitan church. We have singles' classes for adults who have never married and solos' classes for those who are single again. Our large congregation also meets twice a month in small home churches in order to minister better to individual needs. There are plenty of small group opportunities, and one can easily get lost in our Sunday morning congregation of two thousand. But for all the social and cultural differences between this church and a little, rural church, I still find women responding much as I did long ago. Without their men, they are uncomfortable and reluctant to take part.

I know both from experience and from talking to hundreds of women through the years that even something as simple as a church-wide potluck dinner can be painful for a woman who is spiritually alone. Maybe you, too, can identify with the following example.

It was even more rushed and hectic that Sunday morning than usual. Not only did Susan have to get herself ready, she had to get the children going without help. Food had to be prepared to take to the church dinner, but she also had to make sure John's dinner was ready for him. John Jr. was ten years old and picked that morning to rebel. He firmly planted his feet and declared that if Daddy wasn't going, he didn't have to go either. It was a battle royal, but Susan won. When the family got to church, Susan was tense and there was a streak of green bean juice down her favorite skirt.

But by the time Sunday school and church were over, she felt more relaxed. She was hungry and the buffet table looked delicious. She went down the line filling her plate and chatting with the others in line. The three children managed to get all the way to the end of the table without spilling anything, and her youngest child even agreed to eat a vegetable. But as she neared the end of the serving table, that old feeling came back again.

All three children went off in different directions to

sit by their friends. Susan faced a fellowship hall full of couples seated together. She had several friends of her own, but they were all seated by their husbands. The younger single adults were at one table, but she didn't feel she belonged there. She looked around but did not find any of the other women who, like her, had phantom husbands. Besides, when she sat by them, she felt the same way she remembered feeling when girls danced with each other at the eighth grade dance: alone and unwanted.

She sighed deeply, put on a socially appropriate smile, and reasoned to herself that being here was good for the children. Then she sat on the edge of a group of several married couples and tried to enter the conversation as naturally as possible. But inside something was aching. Another little stream of ice-cold loneliness was winding its way across her heart.

A DINNER INVITATION

This book is full of personal examples, but I have wondered if perhaps the following example might best be left out. The reason is that it sounds so much like a complaint or an indictment against the church. In a way, I guess it is. But my reason for including it is not to point a finger of blame or to publicly get even with churches from my past. I tell it because I want the reader to know that even in situations like these, a woman can build a social network and learn to be content.

Bill had dropped out of church about five years before he was killed. As a widow, I attended church for seven more years before I was invited to another Christian's home—a total of twelve years.

I spent the first nine of those years in my home

church. I often invited couples and small groups of married people to my home for meals, hosted church parties, and invited single ladies to lunch. But never once in that time did the children and I receive an invitation in return. Sometimes one of my kids would be asked to visit another kid, but never were we asked to come as a family.

When a move necessitated a change in churches, I visited a few, then joined a conservative branch of my denomination. Even though this church preached the gospel and correct doctrine, the three years I spent there were difficult and depressive. The church was very legalistic and so intent on male leadership that all business and most prayer meetings were "men only" events. But after three years in that church, my family did receive a dinner invitation. It was by accident.

A woman I had been particularly close to had left the church when her husband secured work in another town. This young couple had been a delight to me and had been in my home several times. When they came back for a visit one Sunday, I cornered the wife and invited the family out to dinner. She was glad to accept but had to check with her husband.

As it turned out, while I was inviting her, another couple was inviting her husband to their home. Both of them had accepted invitations to different places for the same meal! It took a few minutes to untangle the mix-up, then the gracious hostess invited the children and me to join everyone at her home. At the same time, however, she also expressed concern that the chicken she had prepared might not be enough to go around. No problem! I was glad to pick up a bucket on my way to the house! It turned out to be a beautiful afternoon, yet I couldn't help but realize that the only invitation my family had received in twelve years was by accident!

The next year, I changed church membership. The second Sunday I visited Trinity, my new church, my Sunday school teacher *willingly* invited my family to his home for Sunday dinner. I couldn't believe it! He regarded my teenage children and me as a family unit and asked my family to spend time with his family! I joined the church the next Sunday. I knew I had found a home and stayed at Trinity until another move uprooted me again.

PRIDE, FEAR, SELF-PITY

I mentioned earlier in this chapter that loneliness could not be entirely blamed on either our men or our church. Yes, they do both play a part, a big part. But it is only a part. The spirit inside us and our own will are also factors. Outside forces may make good social interactions harder, but there are also decision and power inside us that help us make the best of the situation we have been given—and to do it without bitterness.

Looking back on my own life, I can clearly see that sad and angry young mother I once was. The Lord battled long and hard before I was finally able to risk taking some responsibility for myself and reach out socially.

When I viewed myself as a helpless victim, I found it gave me a strange mixture of pain and comfort: pain as I sank deep in self-pity and rehearsed my woeful lot in life over and over again, and comfort because revenge is sweet. It was like saying to my husband, "See how miserable I am? I am going to keep it up and pay you back for not acting like I want you to." Revenge can be temporarily satisfying!

But when I took life as it was handed to me instead of insisting that it shape up into what I wanted it to be,

new possibilities opened up and the ice of loneliness
began to thaw.

Of course, it would have been great if life had just
rearranged itself to meet my specifications, especially
since many of my specifications and God's ideas of how
things should be run are the same. If churches would all
be sensitive to the social needs of women alone, if
neighbors would all be friendly, if relatives would all be
ready to welcome and encourage a woman socially, if all
men would be godly leaders who could see the social
and recreational needs of their wives and families as
important, and—most of all—if we women were mature
enough spiritually and emotionally to accept invitations
as a single without feeling like a zit on the complexion
of society, things would be great! But, in our fallen
world, life just doesn't always turn out that way.

When a woman begins to take responsibility for her
own social welfare (and usually that of her children),
she does not have to change her mind about how things
should be. She can still hold to the same ideals and
know there might be a better society if everyone would
just do things God's way. But while holding to these ideals, she must also recognize reality and respond to the
real situation she has been given rather than sit and
grieve because things are not as they ought to be.

IDEAS THAT HAVE WORKED FOR ME

For me, the hardest step was simply crawling out of
that corner and laying bitterness aside. But once I was
willing to work with reality and let my situation be less
than ideal (if that was what God had allowed for my
life), then things began to look up and slowly my
isolated life began to change. By this time the prairie
was far behind me, we had four children, and we were

living just outside a small (very small!) town in East Texas.

My first concern was my children. I wanted them to know the fun of playing in a public park, have the chance to check out books from a public library, be able to read a menu, and know how to find a rest room in a public place. But they had never had an opportunity to learn any of these things, and I was not sure how to change things. Following a pattern I have often used since then, I decided if I didn't know where to start, the first step was to find someone who did know and ask questions!

I cornered a deacon one Sunday while we were struggling with the choir robes and asked him where a good place was to go fishing or swimming. It turned out that good fishing spots were not good swimming spots and vice versa, but when I explained that I wanted to find a place to spend the day with my children, he brightened up and immediately had the ideal suggestion. The local state park was not far away, and it was the best place around for an afternoon of family fun in the great outdoors.

Looking back, it seems amazing to me as I remember the courage and determination it required to take that first step of creating a family outing without the help of my husband. I was frightened to the depths of my soul.

First, there were several days of prayer as I considered how best to approach the subject with Bill. Would he give us permission to go? Would he resent my taking this step without him?

Bill had chosen a life-style of working two jobs plus running our cattle ranch. Although this arrangement left no time for me and the children, I needed to respect his right to choose that way of life if he judged it best. Before I could even approach the subject of my taking the children to the park for a day, I needed to let go of the bitterness I felt and stop expecting him to provide something for the family that he had chosen not to provide at that time. Only after I had taken that step could I expect the Lord to work in his heart so he would give me permission to try creating a recreational time without him.

Once permission was secured, I faced a new and unexpected problem: my own fear. I had seldom driven very far from home and the park was nearly twenty miles away. What if I got lost? What if we were attacked or robbed—or worse? What if one of the children drowned? What would I do without a husband there to protect me?

It took an extraordinary amount of faith and courage to take that step, but once it was made, many more followed. I ventured out and took the children other places they had never been before and found myself enjoying those times even if I was alone.

Slowly, even my attitude toward church functions began to change. I put out an effort to stop feeling sorry for myself when we attended a church dinner. Instead of rushing off as I had before, I volunteered to help with the dishes and took time to really listen to what other people were saying as we chatted over the sink. What a blessing thirty minutes of adult conversation can be to a woman who lives with only children and a workaholic husband! Soon I felt comfortable inviting other women to my home when their own husbands were working. Once when my husband worked day shifts on Sunday, I even had our pastor and his wife to dinner.

After Bill's death I widened my circle even more. I was hostess in my home for small groups and large groups, children as well as adults. Church parties became events that were enjoyed several times each year. Because I felt married men would be more comfortable in my home if other men were around, I would invite two or three couples at a time, usually for a meal. Although I never received invitations in return, people seemed to genuinely enjoy themselves in my home, and I will probably never know exactly how much good it did my two sons to occasionally have a man around the house as they pressed through their teen years.

I believe few people can appreciate the courage it takes for a woman who has spent many years in the snow to go out and build an acceptable social network all alone. For those who are willing to try building, the rewards can be well worth the struggle.

But it is not enough for a Christian woman to give simplistic answers to complex problems. It is not enough for a Christian woman to simply be brave and free of bitterness, then to go about making a society of her own. That answers part of the problem, but it is only part.

The other half of the problem is the social relationships that must of necessity be a joint venture between husband and wife. She can build her world and be content in it, but she still must deal with those areas where her world joins that of her husband. It is where these worlds touch that social choices become the most complicated of all.

PROBLEMS WHERE THE WORLDS TOUCH

For many Christians, the local church is the main point of social contact. Friendships, social service, personal identity, and spiritual nurturance are all wrapped up in that one place.

When a home is divided and the wife finds her fellowship at the church while her husband finds his at the office or the bar, the contrast between these two lifestyles begins to rip the marriage apart. A woman caught in this position needs to do some very clear thinking about the social choices she must make.

It seems to me that a woman's choices most often fall into one of two categories. The first is the moral choice, and the second is the preference choice.

Moral choices are involved when a husband makes statements like, "If you go to the club with me, I'll only drink a little and come home at a decent hour. But if you don't go, I'll come home so drunk they will have to pour me through the door!" Or, "If you don't go with me to this X-rated movie, I'll find someone else who will!"

Moral choices should be the easiest, but unfortunately, some Christian women find they are not easy at all. One reason for this is that the temptation to do wrong comes wrapped in a sheepskin of responsibility and righteousness. When a husband threatens his wife with a statement like those above, he is doing two things that may strongly appeal to her own flesh nature. First, he is giving her a perfect way to stay "pure" and still be a part of the wild side of life. Second, he calls to her desire for control and tickles her ego into believing that she has more power than God actually gave her.

There is a fascination in sin, and even the Bible admits that it holds a certain pleasure (Hebrews 11:24-26). A husband can appear to give his wife an excuse to join in questionable social activities, because, by doing so, she is looking out for his welfare and keeping peace in the family. But in reality she has been offered an opportunity to act like the adulterous woman in

Proverbs 30. This woman sins and then "wipes her mouth and says, 'I've done nothing wrong'" (Proverbs 30:20, NIV).

If a woman is not careful, she will fall for this trap. She will take part in sin while telling herself that it really doesn't matter because she is doing it for a good cause. This woman will often wake up a year or so later and wonder why her life is in agony and where she went wrong. I guess it is like the old saying "You can't sleep with the pigs and not get dirty." A wife who thinks she can engage in sin "for the sake of my marriage" and still wrap her righteous robes around her and live in peace is sadly mistaken.

Excusing poor moral choices as something done to "help" a husband or to "keep peace" has a second reason for being appealing. It tickles a woman's ego. It is, oh, so easy for a well-meaning Christian woman to say she is doing something or going somewhere to protect her husband and to never see the pride in that statement.

We are acting pridefully when we assume that we hold power over another person's righteousness. When we take on ourselves a responsibility that God reserves for each individual alone, we violate personal dignity. No adult should think himself responsible for the moral choices of another adult.

Such behavior is not only deadly to the wife, it is tragedy to the husband as well. The last thing a rebellious person needs is someone to prop him up and "save" him from the natural consequences of his sin. He must learn to be responsible for himself and to stand on his own. Part of the training God uses to teach people responsibility is to let them suffer the pain brought on by their own sin. If your husband wants to get drunk, tell him that is his choice, and if he passes out on the living room floor, do him a favor: let him lie there (although you may consider throwing a blanket over him to prevent death by pneumonia!).

Above all else, don't go to the bars with your husband because you feel responsible to keep him halfway sober! This same principle applies to pornography, wife swapping, and anything else that a Christian wife has judged to be morally wrong or questionable. Christian women faced with moral decisions need to remember the admonition from 1 Timothy 5:22, "Do not share in the sins of others. Keep yourself pure" (NIV).

A second type of complication created where social worlds touch is the decision of preference. These are not questions of right and wrong necessarily but of likes and dislikes.

Church can be the one place a Christian woman enjoys. It may be a place to meet friends and get some positive feedback when all she hears at home is criticism. As a Christian, she needs the company and support of other Christians to stay strong and grow. Church can even be a place to use her talents and learn to feel good about herself. Then along comes this husband who is a sinner anyway and invites her to go instead to a ball game or on vacation or to her mother-in-law's or to an office party with people she doesn't like. Yuck! What a choice! Personal satisfaction versus yielding to the wants of another!

It may not seem fair, but it is in this very choice that Christian character is built. It is very probable that the uncomfortable dilemma of his wants versus hers will create more true Christian growth than years of sitting comfortably on a church pew. As in all situations, our best guide for a problem is the Bible, and one thing the Bible does *not* say is "Thou shalt be at church every time the door is open and serve on every committee that has a need"! But it does have a lot to say about considering the interests of others (Philippians 2:3-8) and living in kindness (Ephesians 4:32) and showing consideration to others. Peter said a woman would win her husband to Christ by her righteous deeds, not by how many times a week she attends a formal church service (1 Peter 3:1-6).

Being faithful to the formal worship services of God's people is important. It is very difficult for Christians to grow if they place themselves in a total vacuum. When a house is socially divided, there are some important questions that must be answered. How much church fellowship is too much? Where does our obligation as a church member stop and our obligation as a wife take over?

The choices are not always easy, but for the wife who is willing to make them, this is one place where her Christian witness can really shine as she willingly lays down self-fulfillment and yields to the desires of her husband.

FINAL THOUGHTS

There is a certain sense in which all people are created alone and spend their whole lives reaching for an intimacy that never fully comes. I don't think it will come until heaven. Even the best marriages don't provide 100 percent satisfaction 100 percent of the time.

A certain degree of aloneness is a part of every life, but the woman standing in the snow can get stuck in the ice and feel she has more than her share. The good news is that it doesn't have to stay that way. No, she may not have the satisfaction of complete intimacy or find her life bubbling over with dozens of interesting, caring friends who are always faithful and always fill all her needs. But then, that is not true of any life.

A woman *can* find freedom from bitterness, an awareness of where the responsibility of others stops and her own responsibility for personal happiness begins, and a social life that goes a long way toward warming the icy streams of loneliness.

SEVEN
THE LONELY
~~~~~~~~~~~~~~~~~~~~~~~~~~~~~~~~
MARRIAGE BED

Women don't usually bring up the subject of sex until I ask. They talk about other problems first. I guess that's logical because women tend to see the marriage relationship as a whole rather than as many distinct aspects. But when we do get around to the subject, we often find it holds some of the deepest struggles within a marriage and, above all, a loneliness so real it is almost tangible.

For many women, sex is like a barometer that measures the pressures moving against the whole marriage. The exact depth of a woman's loneliness and often a hint about what is creating the loneliness will be clearly seen in the bedroom. If the marriage as a whole lacks intimacy, sex will be mechanical and distant. If the marriage is being pulled apart by a power struggle, power plays will be part of sex as well. If the wife feels disrespected in the marriage, she will feel that disrespect even more acutely in bed. Once in a while we find a bad marriage that claims to have great sex, but that is rare. It is far more common for sex to become the first place that symptoms of trouble become clear.

One reason for this is that God created women as highly sensitive creatures who experience sex in the context of the whole relationship, not in isolation. A woman's ability to respond to her husband and feel the joy God designed to be part of the sexual experience will be influenced by everything from her childhood relationship with her father to her husband's attitude toward her last week when she got a parking ticket. Big things from the past—such as abuse—can create major, long-term problems, but little things that mount up over time can also have a dampening effect on sexual enjoyment. How her husband treated her at breakfast and whether or not he is willing to help get the kids into bed will impact what happens in bed that night.

Additional complications are often created by physical considerations such as a woman's menstrual cycle and PMS. Women are complex creations! In fact, they are so complex that it would be foolish of me to think I could cover the subject in one chapter or even one book. I am not a specialist in this field and would refer my readers with specific problems to the many excellent titles on sexual relations available at your local Christian bookstore.

However, because sexual problems and questions are such a vital part of marriage, this book would be incomplete if I did not attempt to answer a few of the basic questions women face regarding this issue. The brief answers I offer should not be considered the last word on the subject, but I pray that they will prick your heart and mind and that the Lord may use them to point you in the right direction.

I don't see what sex has to do with spiritual things. Aren't these two things so separate that one really has little to do with the other?

The spiritual side of human life has a profound impact on sexual performance. These are not two separate worlds but pieces of an interconnected whole. It is as foolish to put the spirit in a separate category and declare it has nothing to do with sex as it is to put a leg in a separate category and say it has nothing to do with the body.

One place where the connection between the spiritual and the sexual will be evident is in the marriage of a believer and an unbeliever. Good sex is based on good intimacy; the sexual act becomes a meeting of souls as well as bodies. This intimacy can never be as complete as it might have been when a Christian is mated with an unbeliever.

God created humans as body, soul, and spirit (1 Thessalonians 5:23). He also says in His Word that we fallen children of Adam are born with our spirits dead (Ephesians 2:1-5). There is a deep, internal part of everyone born that is empty, dysfunctional, hopeless—in other words, "dead"—and it can only be made alive by the Spirit of God (Romans 8:10). When God's Holy Spirit touches our dead spirit and we accept Jesus as our only hope, we are "born again" (John 3:1-18). At that point we become new creatures (2 Corinthians 5:17). We are different. We are changed. Something new is inside us that has been made alive from the dead.

When a Christian with a body, a soul, and a live spirit tries to create true intimacy with an unbeliever who has a body, a soul, and a dead spirit, a full connection becomes impossible. In this case, the unbeliever will sometimes be both satisfied and frustrated—satisfied because all his/her needs are met, but frustrated because he/she can in no way understand why the other mate insists that something is missing. In the meantime, the Christian often feels like a person with one leg six inches too short; something is out of balance, resulting in a limp in life. If the Christian is also a woman, this situation will be doubly hard and have an even greater impact on the couple's sex life because of her tendency to respond sexually to the relationship as a whole. When his spirit is dead, her libido will take notice.

But the nature of the spirit is not the only spiritual issue that will affect a couple's sex life. Fear, guilt, a willingness to risk, vulnerability, and self-image are all spiritual issues, and they are all basic sexual issues as well. Therefore, it should not be surprising if a woman's perception of her man as someone who fails to take the spiritual leadership of the home has an impact on what she feels in the bedroom. This impact may be slight or it may be great, depending on the strength of the marriage as a whole, but it will almost always be felt to some degree.

Did Adam and Eve have sex in Eden? Was this why God threw them out of the garden?

I know this is the 1990s and my book is written to modern, intelligent women. I know that most of my readers wear skirts above their ankles and seldom go anywhere by wagon train.

But being free from long skirts does not necessarily mean we're free from feeling guilty about sex. I still run into women who emotionally regard sex as something dirty and wrong even though their educated, modern mind tells them it's OK. These women even feel guilty in their marriage relationships and deep down believe that the way to create a kinder, gentler society would be to eliminate sex altogether.

There can be many reasons this is true. For some, it might be childhood training that is still echoing in the adult psyche. For others, it is an attitude that became entrenched after they looked around at all the vile corruption, abuse, crime, and filth that are so often involved in the world's use of sex. But I believe the most common reason for a woman to feel that sex is dirty and sinful is the false guilt brought on when she was violated in one way or another as a child or a victim of rape. Abuse and rape victims often blame themselves for what happened, and echoes of this self-blame can continue right on through marriage.

Sex was a part of God's divine, innocent, original creation in Eden. It was not the result of the Fall nor the reason mankind was cast out of the garden. Before sin became a reality, Adam and Eve were sexually active.

God had made Adam and Eve perfect, naked, and unashamed (Genesis 2:25), and in Genesis 1:22 God told them to be fruitful and multiply. This command was given before the Fall of mankind as recorded in Genesis 3. It would have been impossible for Adam and Eve to carry out God's command to multiply themselves if He had not approved of their being sexually active. The most casual reading of the Bible will show that sex, when kept within the bounds of marriage, is approved of by God. He designed it to be a relationship that is full of respect and mutual consent (1 Corinthians 7:5). It should be a joyful experience that has an element of pure fun (Ecclesiastes 9:9), and full of gentle touching and extended foreplay (Proverbs 5:19; Song of Songs 2:6; 8:3).

I know in my head that God does not condemn me for having sex with my husband, but my heart feels guilty just the same. How will this likely affect our relationship?

Loneliness is almost a built-in guarantee for a woman who struggles emotionally with feelings of guilt over sexual relations. The normal bonding that would occur during good physical relations is blocked, and this very important bridge to intimacy is burned.

There can be many reasons for this lingering guilt: early childhood training, a history of abuse, a consistently negative and overbearing attitude from the husband, misunderstanding of Scripture, or guilt feelings over the fact that Jesus said anyone who married a second time while they still have a living mate is guilty of adultery (Mark 10:12).

I recall one woman whose marriage was destroyed by such guilt. Raised in a good Christian home, she had done everything "right" until she fell in love with a divorced man with two children.

Charlene struggled with Jesus' statement that anyone who married a divorced person committed adultery. She struggled, but she never came to any conclusion. She was not willing to give up the man or even to consider doing so. She was afraid of what she would find if she thoroughly investigated the subject in Scripture, so she didn't decide anything (that action was a decision in itself, but she was never willing to be responsible for it). She brushed the question to the back of her mind and walked down the aisle wearing white.

But like most questions that are buried before they are dead, this one came back to haunt her. Still afraid to face the question honestly, she pushed it out of her mind time and time again. However, it was much harder to push aside her feelings of guilt.

When the guilt became too uncomfortable, Charlene handled it like she did most other problems in her life: she passed the responsibility on to others. Her guilt became her husband's fault. After all, he was the one who had been married and divorced before they met, so he had created the mess. He was the one who was so narrow-minded that he didn't see the value of a celibate marriage.

In time, her blaming him for her guilt problem created another problem: anger. This second problem Charlene also handled passively. Unwilling to confront her husband honestly or even admit to her own negative feelings, she resorted to what we call passive-aggressive behavior. This behavior can best be described by the phrase "I don't get mad; I get even."

For Charlene, the "getting even" strategy was for her to become slower and slower in everything she did. It drove her husband nuts! She was never on time, and getting anywhere with her was a major project. No matter how Ted yelled and threatened, she just got worse. She started taking her Christmas tree down January 2 and did not finish until May!

Finally, the marriage deteriorated into a sham. And the taproot of it all was one woman's failure to face honestly her fear that God might possibly not like her having sexual relations with a husband to whom she was legally married.

Ideally, the decision of whether God approves of remarriage (and the sexual relationship it involves) should be made long before the couple says "I do." If remarriage has already taken place, a decision may still need to be made. The past needs to be dealt with and the holiness of the new relationship accepted or rejected on biblical grounds. We not only need to believe that God approves of sex in general, but that He approves of our personal sexual activity as well. Remember, the worst and most damaging decision you can make is to make no decision.

I have been married to my second husband ten years, and we have two children. My first husband is still

living. Is it wrong for us to have intercourse? Am I guilty of adultery?

You are struggling with a question that has perplexed bigger brains than mine for generations. The first thing I would suggest is a thorough reading of the book *Divorce and Remarriage* by Guy Duty (Bethany House). This balanced work will give detailed examination of specific Scriptures that will help you come to a conclusion based on knowledge, not feeling or convenience.

Also, I would encourage you to separate the two questions you asked and take them one at a time.

As for the first, it is definitely not wrong for you to have intercourse with your own husband. Judging by divorce statistics, first marriages are hard enough, but second marriages are even harder. Don't add to the difficulty by withdrawing sex or wallowing in guilt over a past you can't change.

As for the question of adultery, yes, in my opinion you are guilty. But don't let that throw you for a loop. This sin is not a death sentence. It is a sin, just like any other sin. The same blood that covers one covers all. The solution is confession and allowing Him to forgive us.

I think the best answer I could give will be to share the testimony of someone who has been there.

My mother is the most godly woman I have ever met. She wasn't always that way, but time and Jesus do marvelous things to a willing heart. Her first husband, my father, was an abusive alcoholic and a schizophrenic. After twenty years of marriage, she divorced him when her pastor warned that if she did not do so, he would kill either her or her children.

Six years later she met and married Jim. After a difficult adjustment, they shared several good years

together before he died of cancer. I will let her share
her story with you in her own words.

"When I met Jim, I still had a lot of scars from the
past. I had retreated into bitterness and hardness, refus-
ing even the memories of the horrors of alcohol, drugs,
and abuse.

"Jim and I were Christians, and we wanted the blessings of God on our marriage. We both knew that in
Mark 10:12 Jesus clearly said that those who marry
someone that is divorced commit adultery. We openly
discussed this passage and its possible application to
us. We decided that the words of Jesus were clear
enough, but since our case was different, we married
anyway.

"After the marriage, I found that I had not really settled anything concerning this matter. Every time I read
Mark 10:12 or heard a sermon on that passage—or
even a comment concerning these words of Jesus—I
would feel guilty and begin to justify myself. Or, in contrast, I would just retreat into a haze of procrastination
and refuse to deal with it.

"I knew Jesus as my Savior and God as my Father, but
I did not want to risk hearing what the Holy Spirit
might be saying to me. In the twelve years before Jim's
death, I refused to face the truth of the Word of God as
related to this one area. I read many books explaining
the 'true biblical position' for divorce and remarriage
but never came to a place of peace.

"But God is patient and knew I still needed healing.
The years passed. Jim died. Even then I still needed
God's healing touch concerning this question.

"Ten years after Jim's death, as I was praying for a
young lady who was involved in adultery, I finally heard
the voice of the Holy Spirit calling me to accountability.
I yielded to the Lord and decided to call it what He

called it. I said, 'Lord, I am guilty of adultery. You called it adultery, and I call it what You call it. Forgive me of adultery, self-justification, and exalting my will above Your Word.'

"I received freedom that day—a freedom I had needed for years. I was free from the bondage of trying to explain away the words of Jesus, free from the need of self-justification, and, most of all, free from *guilt*. I really believe that for all those years, God was only wanting me to call it what He called it: adultery.

"I am not saying that those who are in second marriages should get a divorce. If Jim were alive today, I would not leave him. But I know the freedom I received when I agreed with God. I could not receive His forgiveness until I faced and named my sin."

I have been married only five years, but I feel as though our sex life has somehow been cheapened. I am not sure what is wrong, but I feel dirty—like I am selling myself rather than loving him. Is that possible?

Yes. A prostitute is someone who hires her body out for reward. Sometimes the reward is money, sometimes drugs, sometimes apartment rent and clothes, but the results are all the same: She gives sex without regard for personal feelings or self-respect so she gets back something very different from sexual satisfaction.

I believe a wife who has never had intercourse with anyone other than her husband can slip into a mode very similar to prostitution as she uses sex as a manipulation technique to wring what she wants out of her husband. This sinful behavior does not mean that the woman has been sneaking out at night and walking the streets to give sex to strangers for pay. But she may be behaving like a prostitute because she has disregarded personal feelings and self-respect and sold her body for reward.

The pay that a wife may expect to get for sexual favors can be different from that expected by a real prostitute. It may be so subtle in nature that the couple might only be vaguely aware that the payoff system is in place. But one day something deep inside the wife begins to stir, and she complains that she feels like a prostitute even though she may not clearly understand why.

An example of this subtle payoff might be a Christian wife who harbors a deep anger toward a husband who will not cooperate in spiritual matters. We will call her Cheral and her husband Peter. Perhaps their sex life began very well, but through ten years of marriage things have changed. Cheral's anger toward Peter made it difficult for her to respond to her husband as freely as she did in the past. Many nights she would roll over saying she had a headache or was tired, but Peter knew she was really mad because he would not do what she wanted.

For his part, Peter stubbornly planted his feet and became determined that this woman would not control him. But Peter's need for a sexual relationship was still there, and like all humans with unmet needs, Peter's mind set about to connive a way to get the need met. Through subtle and not-so-subtle hints he communicated with Cheral that it was not fair for her to expect him to do what she wanted if she refused to do what he wanted. In time, a swap developed where Cheral gave sex with the expectation that Peter would pay her back by going to church the next morning or attending little Peter's choir recital or fixing the car. Neither Peter nor Cheral was satisfied with this system, and the constant power struggle between them wore the marriage down to a sham. Cheral had cause to complain that she felt like a prostitute. She was one.

Because sex is designed to be a mutually satisfying act, and it is sometimes followed by rewarding experiences, the question of why am I *really* doing this becomes complex very fast. For example, a willing, gentle wife giving exciting sex on Saturday night might encourage a reluctant husband to join the family in services Sunday morning. But how does she feel about herself if the only reason she gave was that she was expecting that payoff? How does she feel if the payoff does not come? It can be difficult to honestly determine whether the act was given for the right reasons (personal desire or a desire to please another) or for wrong reasons (manipulation of others for predetermined gain).

If a wife suspects that she has drifted into the role of a prostitute, the road to recovery is simple: Just stop swapping sex for reward. Simple, but oh, so difficult! Two of the basic forces that draw women into the prostitute role are an unbelievably low self-esteem and a deep fear of men that makes women seek ways to gain power in the relationship. These two things do *not* heal quickly, and because the dynamics that drive the behavior have developed over time, changing the behavior will usually take time as well.

However, it is also true that we can act ourselves into a new way of feeling faster than we can feel ourselves into a new way of acting. If a woman will determine to stop expecting rewards for sexual favors and begin to give for reasons of personal desire and/or a desire to please her husband, the root problems of fear and low self-esteem will begin to heal. When self-respect is raised and fear is overcome by faith, the need to control another by using sex will be resolved.

My husband often wants sex. He even comes home drunk and wants to go to bed with me. I hate the smell of liquor, and my first reaction is to push him away. But my friend says that according to 1 Corinthians 7, my body is not my own; it belongs to my husband for him to do with as he will. I feel as though God only cares about my husband's wants and not mine. I want to obey, but does God really want me to give sex to my husband any time, any place, under any condition? I feel disrespected by both my husband and God.

One of the most common complaints I hear from women is that sexually they feel more like a piece of meat than a wife. They are angry at their situation, but they also feel guilty about their anger and desire to reject their husbands. The devil has too often used this Corinthians passage to rub salt in a wound and make the guilt and anger increase.

An extreme example of this would be a former client who told of hiding under her baby's crib so that her drunk husband could not find her and subject her to another night of abuse and rape. Then, the next morning, she would be torn with guilt over the fact that she had not been as "submissive" as she thought God wanted. For this woman, God was not a refuge in time of trouble but an addition to her terror.

Unfortunately, one of the reasons women sometimes feel this way is how they believe God views them and what He expects of the use of their bodies. One Scripture that can create confusion on this subject is in 1 Corinthians 7, where Paul told wives that their bodies do not belong to them, but to their husbands. When this Scripture is taken out of context and overemphasized, it becomes a problem. This problem is even more exacerbated when a woman is married to a man who seems to demand her body while he won't take time to learn her name. This woman often feels that deep inside her there is a real person crying—no, screaming—to be heard and respected as a human, but all her screams fall on deaf ears. She can't even go to the Lord for comfort because she thinks He would simply point a finger at her and shame her for her non-submissive attitude.

Let me say before I begin this section that I do believe in, teach, endorse, and personally practice all scriptural teaching on submission. Before I became a widow, I practiced a wife's submission to her husband. But when one Scripture is taken out of context and used as a rope of bondage, I get downright angry. This Corinthians passage is so often misused and is such a difficult piece of Scripture that I think it is worth our time to pause for a thorough study.

In 1 Corinthians 7, Paul began his discourse by reminding his readers that in this section of the letter he is answering a specific list of questions they had asked him by letter. By carefully reading each of Paul's answers, we get a pretty good idea what the questions were. It is sort of like playing Jeopardy.

For example, the question for verses 8-9 was something like, Should an unmarried person or a widow seek remarriage? For verses 10-14: Can I divorce an unbeliever if he or she chooses not to become a Christian? For verses 15-16: What are my obligations if an unbeliever divorces me? For verses 17-19: Would yielding to Jewish circumcision make a man a better Christian? For verses 20-24: If I am a slave, should I run away so I can serve the Lord only? For verses 25-40: What about marriages arranged by parents years before they or the children become Christians?

The section of this chapter that deals with sexual relationships between believers is found in verses 1-7. In order to understand the full intent and application of Paul's answer, it becomes very important to decide exactly what question he was answering.

Paul's answer is:

> It is good for a man not to marry. But since there is so much immorality, each man should have his own wife, and each woman her own husband. The husband should fulfill his marital duty to his wife, and likewise the wife to her husband. The wife's body does not belong to her alone but also to her husband. In the same way, the husband's body does not belong to him alone but also to his wife. Do not deprive each other [of sex] except by mutual consent and for a time, so that you may devote yourselves to prayer. Then come together again so that Satan will not tempt you because of your lack of self-control. I say this as a concession, not as a command. I wish that all men were as I am [single]. But each man has his own gift from God; one has this gift, another has that. (NIV)

As we scratch our heads and guess the specific question Paul was addressing, a short lesson in church history may be helpful. The city of Corinth was sexually perverse. There were thousands of temple prostitutes, both male and female. Drunkenness and brawling were commonplace. In fact, the expression *to Corinthenize* became a synonym for our word *orgy*. During this time and later in church history as well, some married couples thought it best to be celibate so they could devote their time and energy to works of charity rather than to family and be an example of self-control to others.

Two problems were created by this decision. First, what if the couple vowed to do that, then three years

later changed their minds? Would it look like they were
being disobedient to the Lord? Second, what if only the
husband or the wife wanted to pursue that kind of life
and the other partner disagreed? I believe questions
about volunteer celibacy in marriage are the only ones
that fit all of Paul's answer.

If these were the questions, it immediately becomes
apparent that these verses have only limited application to normal sexual relations and submission. But
even if I am wrong and Paul had completely different
questions in mind, he still makes it clear that these
verses are not a command (verse 6). Also, his instructions that a wife's body does not belong to herself alone
(verse 4) conversely indicate that it does not belong to
her husband alone. He does not have total ownership,
but his wife also has ownership over her own body. She
is not meat. In verse 5, this same mutual respect is
found when Paul requires mutual consent before sexual relations are stopped for a time of prayer. One partner, no matter which sex, was never given leave to
overpower, demand, and use the other sexually.

**My husband and I are exact opposites in everything. I
don't know how we have managed to survive these past
twenty years. When we were first married, I felt like he
was all over me all the time demanding sex and I hated
it. I was worn out from the kids and just wanted to sleep.
Now the kids are grown, and I am waking up to a whole
new self-awareness. There is no more fear of pregnancy,
and I would like a little sizzle in our romance, but his
company is in trouble and all his energy goes that direction. He is snoring while I am yearning. Any solutions?**

Sexual differences such as you described are very
common. They are also *very* frustrating to those
couples struggling through them.

One thing to remember is that life is seldom fair and almost nothing goes according to plan. If your sex life is going great, there will be a glitch in the machinery somewhere else.

But it is a comfort to know that even in this mismatched, always-broken world, God has given us some principles to work out personal differences. These relational principles can be used to work out sexual differences as well.

Many, many Scripture passages deal with interpersonal struggles, and most of these passages could be applied to the sexual relationship. We could go anywhere in this abundance to find help, but I am going to center on Romans 12:1-15:8. This section is one of the most concise how-to passages in the Word.

I have chosen four basic principles about normal Christian living from this section that I believe can also be applied to the question of sexual conflicts. You may need to stretch a little to see how the principles in these verses can be applied to sex problems, but I believe your efforts will be well rewarded.

Principle #1: I am never expected to do what I cannot do. The longer I counsel the more amazed I am at our ability to take on all kinds of burdens that God never intended for us to bear while at the same time avoiding the responsibilities we need to pick up. One example of this is the unnecessary stress we sometimes live under when we think another person has rejected us or disagrees with us. We can go on a guilt trip for weeks because we can't make the other person change. If that person doesn't like us, our world turns totally upside down. We are almost driven to force them to make peace with us, and if they refuse, we feel guilty.

In Romans 14:19 we are told to make every effort to do those things that lead to peace, but we are also told that our responsibility to make peace is limited. "If it is possible, as far as it depends on you, live at peace with everyone" (Romans 12:18, NIV). Note that Paul did not say it was our job to make other people peaceable and happy. We can't do that. Our job is to make peace only as far as peace depends on us. We have a limit. God does not expect us to do the impossible.

Often the most hopeful statement clients can make is, "I am so sick and tired of butting my head against a wall. I just want to give up and quit." When I hear that, my heart beats a little faster, and I suspect we are on the road to recovery at last. If clients want to give up, that's great! Because what they are usually giving up is a determination to control and fix the world. They sweated valiantly trying to make everyone happy; they struggled with all their might to change other people; they manipulated and plotted and tried to force situations. They tried to take on the guilt of the world, and now they are beaten and helpless. I don't wonder that they feel tired; after all, they have been trying to do God's job for Him—and that is a pretty big load to carry!

The good news is that we don't have to live that way. We were never designed to carry the burdens of the world or to be the total all-in-all to another individual. We are limited in our ability to make peace and to supply another's need. We are not responsible for the decisions that other people make. The problem is not that God expects us to do the impossible but that we sometimes expect that of ourselves.

Now let's translate that basic relational principle into the sexual realm. If we have a mate that is either wanting sex when we don't or not wanting sex when we do, there is no peace at that point. We are pulling one way, and our mate is pulling the other. We can apply this first principle by defining our boundaries, taking responsibility for what we can do and recognizing our limitations for what we can't do.

It may be that one thing we can do is to give in to our mate's wishes. There will be more about that aspect in principles #3 and #4. But we also need to recognize our limitations. We cannot take on ourselves the total responsibility for another's sexual satisfaction. There may be things going on inside that person of which we are completely unaware.

An example would be a husband who repeatedly complained about his wife's inability to satisfy him sexually. She carried the guilt and responsibility for his problem for years, only to find later that he was heavily involved in pornography. No one could have satisfied his "need." The guilt rightly belonged to him, not her.

There may also be things going on inside ourselves that limit us. An example of this would be a woman who was sexually abused as a child. At the beginning of recovery, she may truly not be able to respond to her husband in the best way. It may take years before she is completely free to love him as vibrantly as she should.

We must make every effort to live at peace with others, but that effort must be tempered with the knowledge that more is involved than our personal effort. We have our limitations. God sets us free at the point where solving the problem depends on the response of another. He sets us free, and we need to set ourselves free. When you have done what you are capable of doing, let the situation go.

Principle #2: My feelings and desires are important. Another relational principle that we sometimes miss is that self is important and worth consideration. It is pride to put self and personal desires ahead of everyone else, but it is also pride to ignore, beat, and degrade self. The ground is level at the foot of the cross.

No one person stands above another and none stand below.

In Romans 12:3-8 we find a principle about pride and how it impacts personal relationships. Paul begins the passage by saying, "Do not think of yourself more highly than you ought, but rather think of yourself with sober judgment, in accordance with the measure of faith God has given you" (NIV). Unfortunately, a lot of folks read that verse and only see the first part, then spend a lifetime beating up on themselves in an effort to obey Scripture and not think too highly of themselves. Every time they do something right or worthy, they immediately pounce on it with five negatives in an effort to stay humble. But Paul's instruction to us is that we think about ourselves "soberly"—that is, in fair and truthful terms.

A prideful person is someone who has one way of looking at self and a different way of looking at everyone else. If another person makes a mistake, the prideful one sees the mistake as awful and stupid and pointless. But if self makes the same mistake, pride has seventeen dozen different reasons why outside forces are to blame and the action was reasonable under the circumstances.

We see pride in people like these and recognize their double standard, but do we also recognize the double standard of pride when the coat is put on backward? It is also pride when the mistakes of others can easily be forgiven, but mistakes made by self must bring shame for months; when others can be encouraged, but self must make it on its own; when others can be given credit for what they do right, but self must never feel good about a job well done; when the wants and needs of others are perfectly legitimate, but the wants and needs of self must never be acknowledged.

Christians talk a lot about the need to eliminate pride from their lives. I agree. We should talk about it and fight pride in all forms, but I fear that in our zeal to eliminate pride, we have erred on the other side. We have not so much eliminated pride as learned to brag on it when it is running in reverse gear.

As I mentioned before, self-esteem is not only a spiritual issue, it is also a sexual issue. Part of self-esteem is self-respect. We need to respect our feelings and desires just as much as we respect those of another—not more, not less. The standard we use for others is the same standard we use for self. We are not above anyone, but we are not below others either. Our mate's desire to have sex or not to have sex should be a real consideration for us but not the *only* consideration. Our feelings matter as well.

Principle #3: I am free to choose to meet your needs from a pure heart. Romans 15:2-3 gives us a principle that in East Texas slang is a "bugger-boo" (big, ugly, and tough). Paul said, "Each of us should please his neighbor for his good, to build him up. For even Christ did not please himself" (NIV).

The thing that makes this simple statement so complicated is human nature. We have trouble enough knowing our own minds, much less our own hearts. We say we are doing a thing to please and build up another person, then that person somehow displeases us or doesn't respond according to our expectations, and our emotional reaction tells us that at least part of our motive for giving was to please ourselves. We give our time and energy to sing in the choir because we want to serve the Lord, but when we are not picked for the solo part in the cantata we want to pick up our music and go home. We take the neighbor children to church because we long to see them saved, but after we have been doing this for three months and no one has dramatically given their lives over to the Lord or complimented our kindness, we grow tired, feel unappreciated, and quit. When we feel like this, we should ask ourselves: Was I really seeking to please my neighbor for his good, or was I seeking my own good and pleasure?

Translating that principle into the realm of sexual relations, both the instruction and the complication become clear: If I have a mate that wants sex more often than I do, I should yield and please him, not just myself. If I have a mate that does not want sex as much as I do, I should yield to that desire and not pressure or demand what he is uncomfortable giving. Yet while I am doing these things, I must be doing them from a position of spiritual strength and self-respect, not because my desires are unimportant or because I am my spouse's slave or because I need to get back a reward.

That is not an easy assignment! It is a balancing act that requires a lot of time and practice. I believe one key to achieving that delicate balance is knowledge of my freedom of choice. I know that choice best when I remember whose servant I really am.

Principle #4: I am the Lord's servant, not man's. One of the sweetest times of personal freedom for me came when I realized that I was not the servant of other people, I was the servant of the Lord. God alone was my boss. I might carry out His request by serving the people in the church or the people in my home, but I was *not* their servant!

Paul approached this subject in Romans 14:1-18. He had two groups of people casting stones at each other because their ways of doing things were different. Each group was convinced they were right, and if they were right, the other group obviously had to be wrong. But Paul's amazing answer to these antagonists was that they were both right.

That idea makes some Christians very nervous. When they try to think of two opposite things that are both right, it absolutely blows their minds. They see everything in life as being either in the box or out of it. To even hint that there are times when things are both in and out is a real stretch for them.

Paul explained that both of these groups were doing what they were doing as a service to their Lord Jesus. Each group stood alone before its Master. This gave them the freedom to be very different from each other but both right. It even gave both the freedom to change their way of doing things in order to conform to the desires of another without being hypocritical. They were each free to choose because they were the Lord's servants, not the servants of the opposing group.

I can see two ways this relational principle can apply to the sexual realm. The first is our obligation to recognize that different is not always wrong. The second is the freedom we obtain when we view ourselves as the Lord's servants, not as slaves to each other's whims. Knowing that we are God's servants, not man's, gives us a freedom that can probably best be explained by example. In this case, I know no better example than a letter I have from a woman we will call Carol.

"As far as sex goes, I don't know when things began to change for the better between John and me. It took a long time. The truth is that most of the changing was somewhere deep inside me. I had always given sexually, but I resented it. I felt abused and degraded. Now I still give, but I either find a degree of satisfaction in pleasing him, or sometimes I even enjoy it for myself.

"I was sexually abused as a child, and that had a big

impact on my relationship with John. From the earliest days of our marriage, I seemed to be two different people at once when it came to sex. When we were out in a group or when John was not paying attention to me at home, I was very aggressive sexually and would tease him or openly flirt with him. But the moment John would get serious, I wanted him to stop. In therapy I realized it was my desire for power over a man that made me so aggressive, and both my need to be in control and my fear of men that made me turn cold at the last moment. It was a problem that seemed to have no answer, and it almost wrecked our marriage.

"When the therapist asked me to think about the possibility of giving sexually as a service to the Lord, I responded with a nervous laugh. That seemed embarrassingly wrong. I served the Lord by doing good deeds, and I could never think of sex as 'good.' But I tried to do as he suggested.

"Slowly, I found that I was changing inside. I still had many of the same emotions that I had before, but as the power was taken out of my hands and put in the Lord's, I was more willing to respond to John's feelings. And as I served God, not John, I realized John was not in control and I was doing this because I chose freely to serve the Lord by serving him. Then the fear was much less.

"I am still working on it, but I can honestly say that sex is now a bonding and enjoyable part of our marriage, not a burden."

My husband has had health problems for the past few years. His medications and weakened condition along with his concern about overexertion have caused our sexual relations to become less and less frequent. It has now been five months since he expressed an interest in physical love. I am healthy and in mid-life. Frankly, I miss sex, and I have real needs. I feel cheated, angry, and lonely. I know God doesn't want me to have an affair, but what else can I do?

The first thing you can do is to recognize that your situation is neither that unusual nor that desperate.

It is a normal experience to be celibate at certain times. These are most often brief periods, but they require the same discipline and self-control as longer periods of abstinence. Childbirth, business trips, military assignments, marital arguments, illness, mood swings, and certain medications can all be reasons for abstinence in marriage, and we haven't begun to consider those who have abstinence forced on them by divorce or death or those who remain single and celibate by choice. One way or another, almost all Christians experience living without sex in a body that strongly disagrees with that decision!

These are normal and natural times that almost everyone goes through, but they can also be difficult times. In some cases, very difficult.

I believe the most difficult situation is when a person has been sexually active and, for one reason or another, is forced to stop. This may happen when a person is touched by God's grace and saved and suddenly realizes that a change of moral code forces a change in sexual behavior; or when a death or unexpected divorce causes a sudden switch from having plenty of sex to having none; or when an illness takes away what should have been the sexually most active years; or when our mate wants to stay married but turns sexually cold.

Having been through the situation of my husband's sudden death, which created celibacy for me, I have a great deal of compassion for others in similar circumstances. But my word of encouragement to them is that no one has ever yet died from abstinence! You may wonder about that statement if celibacy is a new experience for you, but hang in there. The first six to nine months are the hardest. However, there are things we can do to make those months and the months that may follow easier to manage.

First, expect your body to act like a body. It is not a brain. It is not a spirit. It is a physical body and will physically react. I have talked with many divorcées, widows, or lonely wives whose sex life at home is the pits who have been shocked by what they felt when the boss was leaning over their shoulder explaining a new procedure or when the pastor warmly took their hand at the door after Sunday services. Even women who always thought they did not like sex sometimes get caught off guard by strong, physical sensations.

These feelings do not mean you are evil or even that you have sinned. They are most often simply feelings over which we have limited control that will come and go at various times and in different circumstances.

These feelings can lead us to sin in several ways, but the feelings themselves are not sin. They become sin if we seek after them and try to make them happen again and again because we enjoy the sensation. They can lead us into physical adultery. They can cause us to dwell on mental pictures that are adulterous. They can cause us to defraud the men around us as we flirt to create tension and desire, then turn their propositions down at the last moment because we are "obeying" the Lord.

We have almost no control over circumstances that barge into our life and make celibacy a necessity and only limited control over the physical feelings that arise, but we do have some control. It is that area of control I would like to encourage.

Any woman who lives without sex and is struggling should make it a practice to find out what turns her on and then turn that thing off. Of course, the obvious things, such as sexy movie scenes or steamy novels, should be avoided at all cost. These things can be as addictive as street drugs. This category also includes soap operas.

There are also other, less obvious things that trigger sexual arousal. These will differ from one individual to the next. It may be Christian romance novels or country music or a cartoon movie of Cinderella. But whatever it is, you will know if it is a problem by what happens next. If it stirs physical feelings that are hard to control or makes you angry over what you are missing in life or turns your attention to daydreams about the guy who works in the next office or sets you thinking about the broad shoulders of your best friend's husband, avoid that thing like a disease.

No matter how careful we are, feelings will sometimes come, and it will be impossible to avoid everything that triggers them. One day something may be only a pleasant diversion that simply makes you feel warmly romantic, and another day that same stimulus may create feelings that have you climbing the walls. There will be times when situations or thoughts or people catch you by surprise with intensely sexual feelings and other times when for long periods you may feel as though you are of neuter gender as far as sexual matters are concerned. But don't volunteer to make matters worse for yourself when you have the option to avoid the trouble before it begins.

Another thing to remember is that the ability to be celibate and at peace is a gift we can ask God for. Paul referred to that life-style as a gift he had from God, and he recommended this way of living to others. Just as the gifts of prophecy or tongues or giving are gifts of God, so the ability to be celibate is from God (1 Corinthians 7:7). Jesus implied the same thing (Matthew 19:11-12). If every good and perfect gift comes from the Father of light with whom there is no shadow of turning (James 1:17), and if we are put in a situation where the gift of celibacy is what we need, I don't think it is at all inappropriate to ask God for that gift (James 4:2-3) and expect Him to give it.

One of the loneliest places in the world can be a double bed. Sometimes it is lonely because there is no one on the other pillow. Sometimes it is lonely because the person on the other pillow doesn't care, can't understand, demands too much, doesn't know our name, or simply can't give us what we need.

But none of these things needs to grow so large that it blocks all joy or peace from our lives if we are willing to be first and foremost women of God. The world and everything in it—even our husband—must be secondary. Even our own comfort and satisfaction must come second to the call of God. When that happens and we reach that pliable, yielded state, we will find that our loneliness is secondary, and life is in balance again.

EIGHT

HOW CAN I

RESPECT A WORM?

One of the instruments that I use to counsel married couples is a written exam that asks them to circle phrases that apply to their marriage. One of the phrases, "I feel unrespected by my mate," is almost always marked by one or both spouses. Yet that problem is seldom mentioned by the couple during an oral interview. It is as if they never thought of using the word *unrespected* to express how they felt until the paper suggested it. It also seems to me that once they have been introduced to the word, men are a little more likely to use the term whereas women are more likely to use *unloved* to describe their feelings.

I think this is significant when we consider that one of the most commonly known Scripture passages on the marriage relationship uses these same two terms. It is Ephesians 5:33, and it instructs a man to love his wife as much as he loves himself and tells a wife that she must see to it that she respects her husband. Love is what the husband is to give the woman, but respect is the woman's obligation to her husband.

This verse is often taught in marriage seminars, and

most Christian women who have searched the Word for answers to their problems have read the verse more than once. But I wonder how much of that teaching has soaked down to the heart? Do we realize how vitally important it is for a wife to feel as though she is loved and a husband to feel he is respected? Or is the problem not so much that we wives don't know we ought to respect our husbands as it is that we lack the skills to do so when we feel the man has not earned our respect?

I was slated on a seminar program a few years back with several people who had their Ph.D.'s, and I felt very much outranked by both my companions and the situation. I had not even finished my master's degree at the time.

As the program ended, we formed a panel and fielded questions from the audience. The questions were simple enough at first, but then a dark-haired woman who appeared to be in her late thirties took the floor and things got complex. She was in control of herself, but it was easy to hear the strain in her voice as she choked back the tears and asked us "experts" how to handle the problem that was breaking her heart.

This woman had three sons. Her husband had left her two years before and chosen a completely different life-style than the one she lived and hoped her sons would adopt. He had been a moral and even godly man when she married him, but he began drifting from the things of God and then living in outright rebellion. Now he was heavily into drugs and alcohol and had a live-in girlfriend. He also had visitation rights to her sons.

She longed to see her boys grow into stable, well-adjusted men who felt a dignity and pleasure in their own manhood, and she had invested a lot of time in studying how she could help them. Everything she read said that the best thing she could do was to teach her boys to respect their father and show that respect herself. If she belittled and condemned their father, the boys would identify with him and begin to doubt themselves as male. The question was, How could she show respect for their father and encourage her boys to feel good about maleness without seeming to approve of the life-style her husband had chosen?

WHAT'S A WOMAN TO DO?

I was not really pleased with our answers that day. We sounded trite. The woman's question stayed with me for months. I felt we as "experts" had committed the same sin that the book of James mentions when a hungry man approaches a Christian for help and the Christian says, "Go, I wish you well; keep warm and well fed," but gives the person no practical assistance (James 2:14-17, NIV). What *could* this woman do?

For that matter, what can thousands of women do? Some face situations like this mother. Others face circumstances that are less dramatic but just as confusing. What about the pastor's wife who knows her husband cheats on his expense account? Or the young wife who thought she had the perfect husband until she found a pornographic magazine under his car seat? What about the general lack of respect that is fostered when a husband leaves his body at home but emotionally lives in another world—and all the tiny pieces of neglect and irresponsibility add up through the years?

In situations like these, God's instructions to a wife that she respect her husband become a very big problem. How can we respect the unrespectable?

Allow me to assume the worst. To really demonstrate what I want to talk about in this chapter, let me pick a situation that is probably far worse than the one you face. Let's pretend that you are married to a king-sized, first-class, grade-A slob. This character thinks it is funny to belch at the table. He constantly wears a grimy cap that has I Like Sex written across the brim. He is a cheat and a liar. He hasn't seen the inside of a church in ten years, and his capacity for selfishness would make Narcissus envious.

Let's further assume that you are very righteous and pure. You serve the Lord fully and want to obey Him in all ways. Then someone like me comes along and reminds you that the Bible says you are to respect your husband, and, as far as it depends on you, to teach your children to respect him, too. I pull out a Scripture that slaps you right in the conscience and you stare at me in disbelief. How could the Lord possibly expect you to respect that ignorant, selfish pig of a man? After all, he has not earned your respect. If anything, he has made the idea of respecting him a mockery. How can God command a woman to do something like that?

Well, let's put the shoe on the other foot and reframe the problem before we attempt to answer it. Can God be fair and command a man to love his wife even when she has not earned it? Could God provide the power for him to love her even when she is not worthy of that love? Did I hear you say, "Yes, but respect is different from love"? True. But I suspect that one is no more difficult to give than the other when our hearts are weary and the mate in question is not cooperating.

Perhaps part of the solution for giving both love and respect to those who are unworthy is a very close definition of the terms. We need to move them out of the realm of being solely emotional in nature and move them into being behavioral. Both respect and love can be ways that you feel, but they also can be ways that you act and things that you do.

I would like to suggest four behaviors in this chapter that we can choose to do or, in some cases, choose not to do, that will help us to show respect with our actions. You can give this kind of respect no matter how much your man does not deserve it and no matter how much your emotions rebel. You can always set your heart to behave in right ways that demonstrate respect.

It may be that your husband fits the slob description above or that your respect for him has slowly eroded over time as you found the man you once idolized has clay feet. The fact remains that the Bible says you must respect him, and God never gave a command without providing the power to obey it. How do you do that? By (1) behaving toward him with old-fashioned manners and courtesy; (2) appreciating and verbally expressing the positive things about him; (3) accepting his negative realities; and (4) letting God change your heart until you see your man through Jesus' eyes.

MISS MANNERS WAS RIGHT ALL ALONG

I was in my daughter's kitchen not long ago talking with my youngest grandchild. Beth is six years old and has clear blue eyes and long blond ringlets in her hair. She looks like a porcelain doll and thinks like Tom Sawyer.

One of the passions of her life has been bugs. As a baby she ate anything she could catch. Now she has progressed to capturing the critters. She was very intent on showing me her latest collection, and I asked her if she had named any of them yet. "No," she sweetly replied. Her mom was rinsing dishes at the sink and prompted, "No, what?" Beth gave a deep sigh and said, "No, ma-a-am," drawing out the last vowel to accent her obedience.

I really admire the way my daughter is raising her kids. She does a better job than I ever did, and part of the improvement has been her return to some of the little courteous manners that at one time marked our society. In my younger days I regarded such things as little more than fancy lace on society, but time has given me a different view. I now see them as small, necessary demonstrations of respect that help us honor one another and keep society from going crazy.

As simplistic as it may sound, old-fashioned manners are one way of showing respect. They are not something we feel. So it is not hypocritical to do these actions while we don't feel a thing.

Unfortunately, we women have been quick to notice when husbands fail to do little mannerly things for us—such as pull out our chair, open our door, help with our coat—but very slow to recognize our own failures to honor him in small ways. Have you taught your children to say sir when referring to their father? Have you by example and instruction shown your children they should not interrupt Daddy when he is speaking? Once upon a time, there was significance in seating Daddy at the head of the table. How many times have you stated in front of the children and to your husband's face that you didn't have two children, you really had three, because he was as much a child as any of the others? We are commanded by our Lord to respect our husbands, and one way to start is through dusting off our manners.

One of the first places a wife may find her manners lacking is in her public criticism of her husband. I am convinced that a fast track to Christian maturity is to develop the habit of listening to ourselves talk. If the Lord would play back for us at the end of each day the tone of voice and the content of the statements we have been spitting into the air, many Christians would spend a lot of sleepless nights. Think for a while about what you have said about your husband this week to your neighbor and the kids and your mother. Would you have talked about a friend that way? Would you change your tone of voice if Jesus were on the extension phone? Would you have spoken that disrespectfully about a neighbor you hardly know?

Using cutting remarks and looks of contempt that are displayed in front of the children or other adults is like throwing acid in the face of a marriage. These are quickly picked up by the kids and become the building blocks of disaster in the home as respect for the father is eroded.

I remember an example of this acid at work in a family that spent the night with us. We did not know these people intimately, but they were friends of friends at church who needed a place to sleep while passing through town.

It was Sunday afternoon, and in the relaxed hours after lunch, the father of the family stretched out on the sofa to watch a ball game and fell asleep. The man had a rather large beer belly left over from his wilder days, and as he slept his shirt crept up, exposing the lower half. His wife and I were also in the living room visiting and had not noticed the exposed paunch.

This man's teenage son entered the room and snorted his disgust when he saw his sleeping father. "What a fat pig he is," the boy said with a sneer. "He is such a slob!"

I expected the mother to react negatively to her son's comments. Instead she shrugged her shoulders and gave a quick, sheepish grin. It was obvious that the boy was only repeating what he had heard his mother say many times, and she dared not correct him without changing her own behavior.

Normal manners can go a long way toward teaching children to respect their father, but these must be modeled as well as given by instructions. We model respect in two ways. One is the way we treat the child's father, the other is how we respect the child himself. We teach children to respect the property, uninterrupted speech, and ideas of the adults around him by respecting the child's property, speech, and ideas.

Children can be taught manners even when they are older. However, it probably would *not* be a good idea to try to totally change yourself and the children all at once. A kid that has been saying, "Yeah, whaddaya want?" for ten years will likely find it impossible to twist his tongue around the word *sir* without choking. But if a wife will pick one or two small items of respectful behavior (especially if they involve changing only her own behavior) and master those before moving on, she can slowly build the mannerly demonstration of respect back into the family structure.

APPRECIATING THE POSITIVE

While it is possible to respect someone even when he doesn't deserve it, it is a whole lot easier if we can find something—*anything*—that is positive about him. But looking for something positive may be like searching for a black cat in a dark room. It takes a lot of effort and a special kind of sight adjustment. My experience has been that the biggest block to seeing the positives in another person (particularly one that I am not getting along with!) is self-pity. When I concentrate on myself, I am so centered on the negative feelings inside me that

I immediately reject any hint of good I suspect in the other person.

To me, self-pity feels warm and muggy, like a swamp. The mist and steam is all around, clouding everything else from view. I crawl into a corner of my makeshift lean-to, curl up in a fetal position, and suck on a sour stick. If anything positive or anything that used to bring me pleasure comes drifting into the periphery of my vision, it is like a tiny butterfly, and my immediate reaction is to crush that disgustingly lovely thing to make it as miserable as I am. I don't want a positive! I like my swamp!

At times it has been a real challenge for me to allow a positive in myself or anyone else. I would rather pity myself and concentrate on how sticky it is in my swamp. If I allow myself to feel something good or pleasurable, I lose my excuse for staying where I am. And besides all that, the butterfly is such a tiny, useless thing. My swamp is big; it's my daily reality. Why should I let such a tiny, fleeting thing steal my excuse for misery? It can be like prying open a rusty can to get my soul cracked wide enough to *feel* the presence of a tiny positive.

There are probably some tiny positives floating around your husband that you have ignored for a long time. Maybe he is a workaholic, but he does provide a living. Maybe he hasn't been to church in ten years, but he keeps the car in good repair. Maybe he is undisciplined, irresponsible, and fifty pounds overweight, but he looks great in a bow tie. I have no idea what the positive aspects of your husband are, but if you will look long enough and pray hard enough, you will find a few lying around somewhere.

Once you have found these butterflies, don't stomp

them out of existence. Do something with them that may help encourage feelings of respect to blossom.

My first suggestion would be that you put them on a list and keep them close by your Bible. Each day when you pray, thank God for the positives. Get in the habit of praise.

Also, let the positives come out of your mouth. Listen to what your own voice is saying about your husband as you talk with family and fellow church members. I know it may be hard to naturally work "John looks great in a bow tie" into the conversation, but try it. You might even mention a positive out loud to your husband!

You don't have to work up false feelings or say things you don't mean in order to respect your husband. You can follow biblical directions to respect him by simply accepting the possibility that there might be a positive somewhere in his life and then verbalizing that positive.

ACCEPTING THE NEGATIVE

When I encourage women to accept the negatives about their husband, I do not mean they should take part in his sins or approve of what he does. There is a difference between acceptance and approval. Acceptance is to admit a truth that is already there. Approval is to say the truth is good. For this section, the behaviors that help create respect for the man of the house will not be so much what we specifically do, but what we don't do.

First, *don't deny the truth*. If Daddy is drunk, don't tell the kids he is sick. If he cheats on his expense account, don't pretend you don't know. This calls for a great deal of wisdom as we strike a balance between those times when love openly speaks the truth (Ephesians 4:15) and is discreet enough to cover another's shame (Proverbs 10:12; 1 Peter 4:8).

We first need to admit the truth of any negatives to ourselves and then never hide our knowledge from our mate. Trying to "protect" our children or other close family members by giving out lies and half-truths leads us to walk in sin. Such behavior will complicate rather than help our problems.

There are ways to speak the truth and still show respect and love. If the truth is that Daddy is in bed with a hangover, throwing up and growling at everyone who tiptoes past his door, it would be disrespectful to tell his eight-year-old son, "That bum of a father of yours is drunk again." But it is also a lie to tell him, "We need to be quiet this morning because Daddy is sick with a tummy ache." Instead, the mother might say something like, "Daddy drank too much alcohol last night, and it made him feel bad." Under certain circumstances she might even go so far as to say, "It was Daddy's own choice to do this, and he is responsible, but we can choose to help him feel a little better by being quiet this morning."

A common family dysfunction is sometimes called the elephant-in-the-living-room syndrome. That is a situation where something is badly wrong and everyone in the family system knows it, but there is an unwritten rule against talking about the problem. It is as if the family has a huge elephant sitting in the middle of their living room, but they all walk around the beast and pretend he isn't there. The name of the elephant may be alcoholism, child abuse, intense anger, or hatred between a mother and father, but no one admits to what is going on. This game of pretending has developed over time to help the family deal with pain, but instead of making things better, it makes them worse. We accept a negative in ourselves or some-one else by admitting that the problem is real and bad and part of our lives, not by pretending it doesn't exist.

Accepting someone's negatives is a vital element of respect. When we view someone as without fault and emotionally respond to his perfection, we are engaging more in worship than in respect. If we refuse to admit any faults that another person may have, we are not respecting him. We are responding to a false image that we have built in our mind.

One of the ways we need to accept our mate with all his faults still attached is in the area of spiritual leadership. I often hear women moan that they don't have a leader in their home because their husband is not a Christian or he is not performing up to the standard they have set. The woman feels she could do so well if only she had a leader.

I am quick to point out that she *does* have a leader. He may be a lousy leader, but he is *her* leader. Just as surely as our country has a president even if he is a bad president, a family has a leader even when he is a bad leader. Just as I owe my president respect because of the office he holds—even when I don't agree with him and am sure that a blind monkey could do a better job—so I owe my husband respect for the office he holds. I need to accept him as my leader even if he is far from what both God and I would want him to be.

Not only must we first stop pretending that negatives aren't there, but, second, we must also stop making excuses for the negatives when we see them. *Don't make excuses* for the negative behavior of your husband.

I am sometimes amazed at the lengths to which people will go to keep from putting the responsibility where it belongs. A wife may blame her husband's boss for being unreasonable when he fires John just because he showed up late for work nine times in two weeks! It is always the fault of the circumstances or the fault of the way his parents raised him or the fault of the church or the fault of the weather, but—in his wife's eyes—it is never John's fault.

One reason we try so hard to prove that our husband has no real flaws is that we have built our security and/or reputation on his perfection. The same is true of our need to blindly look past a problem in our children, family of origin, or pastor. If they have a flaw, then we are threatened. We see this in a mother who may not be able to accept the idea that her son is in trouble with the police. She insists that the policeman has singled her son out as an example and is being unfair because if her son is bad, then she may be a bad mother. If the cop is bad, her reputation as a mother is safe.

If a wife has built all of her security on her husband and is depending on him as a life source, she is in danger if he shows a weakness. It may become very necessary to convince everyone, including herself, that the man is wonderful, sinless, and perfect. Any flaw that may crop up is excused and neatly brushed under the rug.

This excuse making is not respect or love. It is shifting blame in an effort to keep ourselves safe. If we want to build true respect for someone, we must not make excuses for his behavior.

A third don't: *Don't take responsibility for your husband.* We dare not take on ourselves the responsibility that rightly belongs to another! A wife who does so becomes the excuse for a man's bad behavior. I know a wife who blamed herself because her husband abused her when he came home drunk and flew into a rage because the top of the refrigerator was dusty; after all, if she would only keep the house clean, he wouldn't have to pull her out of bed and beat her at three o'clock in the morning!

One way we honor people is by holding them responsible. If a rock rolls down a hill and bruises my toe, I can say the rock is to blame for my pain, but I would not say the rock is responsible for it. To be responsible something must be legally or morally answerable (*Funk & Wagnall's Standard Dictionary*, 1980). Only people can be responsible. When I admit within myself that someone is responsible for bad behavior, it is a way of respecting him as being different from a rock.

WHY DON'T YOU PRAY ABOUT IT?

I know that telling someone to pray about a situation is almost a stock answer when all else fails. But I don't make that suggestion lightly. Prayer is the most vital, the most crucial of all Christian endeavors. Without prayer all other activities either cannot exist or are greatly hampered. There is power in prayer.

When we set out to change our heart and actions from disrespect to respect, we have taken on a monumental task. The work often involves changing long-established patterns of thinking and habitual ways of doing things. It involves being vulnerable as we lay down our weapons of verbal revenge and seek to encourage someone who may be doing everything he can to discourage us. It involves loving the unlovable. These are tasks that only God can accomplish. We need His power.

An exercise that folks sometimes find helpful is to go to the place where they do their best thinking. It may be in the car on a long drive, in a quiet room before the fire, in the kitchen as you do dishes, or in bed during those moments just before you fall asleep each night. Relax as much as possible and talk to God for a moment. Ask Him to let you see the world and your mate from His point of view.

Of course, we could never totally see all things as God does because He is God and we are not. Nonetheless, sometimes this simple exercise will help us move a little closer to His view.

Just imagine for a moment that God invites you to step up close to His throne—very close. Maybe you even crawl up in His lap like a trusting child and nestle within His safe and warm arms. Then slowly you turn around and look down. You look across black space to the planet Earth, through blue sky and clouds, and on down to your tiny town. Look at your life as a whole, your house, your mate. How does the view look from God's angle? How does God feel about your mate?

We know a few of His feelings because He told us about them in His Word. We know He sees our mate's life as a whole. The little boy our husband once was is just as real and fresh to God as the man he is now. We know God has a holy, righteous wrath against the sins your husband has committed. We know God has a singular pity as He looks past what your husband does and into the heart of what your husband is. God sees the pride that shows on the outside and the unspoken fear that lives on the inside. If we can but for a moment see our mate as God sees him, our compassion and love and understanding may be changed for a lifetime.

A new view of our mate can only be accomplished as God gives it to us by His grace, and that grace is tapped through prayer. But has your experience with prayer been as difficult and confusing as mine has sometimes been? I have been known to sit in staff meetings with fifteen pastors, and while I listen with one ear to their praying about something that is important, my mind drifts to what I am going to eat for lunch. I kneel because I want to get real serious with God and find my mind concentrating more on my sore knees than on Jesus. I open my eyes after thirty minutes of prayer, and I can't remember a thing I have said. I decide to pray in the morning and oversleep; I decide to pray in the evening and the phone rings off the wall. Then I get an answer to prayer that is nothing short of miraculous, and I want to beat myself because I don't pray more.

Prayer is hard work. But it is also effective work. If a woman seriously wants to obey the command of Scripture that she respect her husband, and if she is convinced that this would be best for both herself and her children, prayer is the place to begin and the place to continue.

I have found that the best prayers are specific prayers. "God, please give world peace" is a good prayer, but "God, please bring peace between John and me when I seek his forgiveness this Thursday at noon" is probably more practical. This specificity is often made easier when we keep a prayer list. In order to put the request on paper, I must box it into words and tame it down to reality. That helps keep my thinking clear and makes it easier to see the answers when they come. A prayer list will also sometimes bring out errors in my approach to prayer. When I read back over my list, do I notice that I am asking God to change everyone but me? Have my requests been balanced with praise?

There is also another way to use a pen and paper to greatly benefit our prayer life. That is to write out our prayers in full.

I remember one lovely young woman whose primary struggle was that she could no longer pray for her hus-

band. This inability to pray added to her guilt and hopelessness. There were many problems in the marriage,
and her pain was so deep it seemed to drown out all
other emotions. Emotions had always been been a vital
part of her prayer life. When there was nothing left but
pain, there seemed to be nothing left with which to
pray. She tried to pray. She wanted to pray. But the
block of pain was simply too big.

Because I felt that her desire to pray for her husband
was real, we tried something different in session. I
handed her a note pad and asked her if she could write
a letter to God, telling Him about her husband and
then making a request to God for him. At first she said
no. This form of communicating with God was foreign
to her. Always before her prayers had been heartfelt
and spontaneous. Writing prayers when no emotion
was involved seemed wooden, unnatural, even false.
But she agreed to try, and within a week she was surprised to find the block to prayer had melted away.

FOLLOWING OUR FATHER'S EXAMPLE

I am convinced that God demonstrates a great deal of
respect for the humans He has created. He does not
regard us with awe; He does not give us a rank we don't
deserve; He does not overlook our sins; He does not
hold us up above Himself. But He does respect us. The
fact that He allows us free will is evidence of that
respect.

As strange as it may sound, God is polite to us and
mannerly. This, also, shows respect. He says in Revelation 3:20, "Behold, I stand at the door, and knock." He
doesn't kick the door in even though He could. He
doesn't slam or insist or force His way. In 1 John 4:16 we

read that God is love, and in 1 Corinthians 13 we are told that love is never rude.

God also freely gives us credit for what we do right. When talking to the churches in Revelation, Jesus always begins with a compliment, if He can, and verbalizes His appreciation of the church (Revelation 2–3). Many feel that the Song of Songs is an allegory of Christ and His Bride, the church. Most of the book is composed of compliments and appreciation verbally expressed between the lover and the beloved.

God also demonstrates His respect by holding us responsible for our sins. He forgives, yes, but He also calls a spade a spade. We are different from the rocks and different from the animals; therefore, we can be held morally answerable for our wrongdoing (Galatians 6:7).

But with all of this, God's final evidence of respect is that He loves us. For some strange reason that I can't fathom, when God looks at us, He looks through the eyes of love and pity (John 3:16). These eyes of tenderness are what we need as we seek to follow His example and His command that a wife must see to it that she respects her husband (Ephesians 5:33, NIV).

NINE

WHEN WOMEN

RAISE CHILDREN

ALONE

When Bill was killed, our two boys were teetering on the brink of puberty. Their older sister, Lori, had for the most part been a joy to raise through her teens. She was a high school senior, and, although I didn't know it then, her college plans would soon change to marriage plans and within two years she would be gone. Their little sister, Nancy, was only eight, and since I had already raised three eight-year-olds, I felt I had a handle on that situation.

But I was soon to find that raising boys was an entirely different story. Raising Billy, age thirteen, and Wesley, age eleven, proved to be one of the greatest challenges, biggest heartaches, and most hopeless puzzles God ever gave me. I have cut hay and vaccinated cows while crying for my sons, enrolled in college in competition with them, and been intimidated by their size and power. I have prayed for them with tears and at times literally begged God to get me out of situations with both my sanity and my family still in one piece. There were problems with the girls—lots of them, but at least with the girls I had some idea of what was going on and what to do next. With the boys, I always felt like I was trying to land a plane in zero visibility, with no instructions from the control tower, while headed for a runway I wasn't sure existed.

Billy was the most difficult of all the children. To the best of my knowledge it was six years after his daddy died before he began to deal with the pain of the death. Until then everything was kept locked tightly inside where the infection slowly ate at his heart.

Outside the home, Billy was a joy to all who knew him—a straight-A student, faithful participant in the church youth group, band chaplain, and a kid who always went a second mile for anyone in need. But once he came home and shut the door behind him, he was rebellion personified. With words and deeds and more words, he let us all know that he couldn't stand the sight of us and what rotten, incapable, stupid people we were. Or at least that is how I and his brother and sisters saw the situation. He might have a different view to share if he ever writes his own book!

At times my frustration with him was so extreme that, I am ashamed to say, I slapped his mouth and bloodied his nose. When he was sixteen, I was pushed to the point of telling him that if he could not show more respect with his mouth and stop making everyone around him miserable, I would find another place for him to live. He chose to stay. When he graduated salutatorian of his class and left for the university, part of my mother's heart was broken because I felt as though I had failed. But another part said, "Thank God and Greyhound he is gone!" And I believe Billy suffered just as much living with me as I did living with him. He felt nearly as good about leaving as I did about seeing him go!

Today Billy is a physicist/mathematician working as

a programming scientist for a major firm in Houston. This same teen who couldn't stand his family is the first to encourage family reunions, call his brother and sisters long-distance just to talk, and ask, "Mom, why don't you find a good man and get married? I worry about you. Do you need any money?"

Not only did Billy turn out to be a reasonable adult, but Wesley and Nancy and Lori are all married and all serving the Lord in their respective churches. At times I shake my head and wonder how on earth I managed to get the kids from point A to point B, and the only answer I have ever come up with is the grace of God plus a faith that simply would not let go of either God or them.

I am really proud of my kids and, I'll admit it, proud of myself for surviving and doing a good job. But that pride is tempered by the fact that I know I am certainly not the first or the last mother to successfully raise kids alone. With faith and guts many women have raised children successfully. Some of these women are modern and have names I know, but one lady who gave me much inspiration when times were tough is from the Old Testament. Her name was Abijah, but I always thought of her as Abi (2 Kings 18:2; 2 Chronicles 29:1).

A MOTHER NAMED ABI

Abi came from a home where God was loved and obeyed. Her father, Zechariah, was one of the priests who advised King Uzziah. She was probably born in Jerusalem during the last years of the reign of this godly king. Her family would have been well off financially and respected in both the king's palace and the higher society of her nation's capital. Isaiah would have been a young prophet at this time. Abi could have led a fairly nondescript, peaceful life except for one thing: her husband.

Like all young girls in Judah, Abi's husband would have been picked for her by her dad. When Zechariah picked a husband for Abi, he made the biggest mistake of her life. Abi was given to Ahaz, a descendant of David and second in line for his throne. After a few quick changes in rulership, Ahaz ended up on the throne and Abi was his queen.

In keeping with the custom of the day and his wicked life-style, Ahaz had other women besides Abi. Even though she was his official queen, she was only one of his many women, and the son she bore him was one of his many sons. She probably lived all her married years without the affection of her husband. Abi knew what it was like to be required to give her life, her loyalty, and her body to a man who could not begin to really communicate with her and did not care to try.

Not only was Abi's home life a mess, her nation was going down the tubes as well. War was bearing down on it from several fronts, and the inept politics of her foolish husband continually made matters worse. When the northern nation of Israel started giving Judah trouble, Ahaz sought help from Assyria. The king of Assyria was glad to agree to "help" Ahaz out by crushing Israel, then he kept right on moving southward until he had reduced Judah to servitude as well. In order to bribe Assyria into some semblance of peaceful coexistence, Ahaz robbed God's temple of both money and costly furnishings, drained the national treasury, and confiscated the wealth of private citizens as well.

But Abi's biggest headache was probably her husband's greed. Ahaz looked at the prosperity of foreign nations and decided to import their gods so that he might prosper also. The ceremonies that were used to worship these gods included temple prostitution and child sacrifice. Ahaz took some of his own sons and burned them alive in order to win the blessings of these gods. Surely Abi must have wondered if her husband's desire for wealth and power would become so great that he would burn her son—the heir to the throne—in an effort to secure favor from these gods.

Abi was trapped in a marriage with no way out. Chained to a monster who had no true godliness about him, she must have often felt her righteous heart would break. There was no security in the nation, no security in her motherhood, no security in her marriage.

It may seem difficult to raise children in our day and circumstances, but how would we like to have walked in Abi's shoes? Is it possible for a mother to raise a godly son when both his father and the nation are corrupt and she is left to do the job alone? Abi did.

Abi's son, Hezekiah, took the throne at age twenty-five after Ahaz's death and led the nation in sweeping revival. His reign lasted twenty-nine successful years, and through him the Lord beat Assyria back behind Judah's borders.

The Bible leaves no doubt that much of Hezekiah's success can be traced directly to the influence of his mother. His godliness and wisdom were not accidents. The Lord even breaks tradition when giving the genealogical records of the kings of Judah and lists his mother's name as well as his father's name (2 Chronicles 29:1). There are not many times when the tradition of listing only male names is broken, and when it is, you can be sure there is something special about that particular woman. Abi is one of these exceptional women.

Getting children from the cradle to reasonable independence is a two-parent job. That is how things are *supposed* to work. All the experts say so. Children need

daddies and children need mamas. It is going to take all
the love, dedication, nerve, brains, and patience that
two well-adjusted adult individuals can pour into those
tiny bodies for eighteen to twenty long years to produce a well-adjusted adult who can in turn nurture the
next generation. But where do these facts leave the
woman who is left to do the job alone?

My heart goes out to any mother who, like Abi, finds
herself in the position of being the one primarily
responsible for the discipline, guidance, and control of
her children, especially if the children are boys.

Not all the mothers who raise children alone are single. Women with military husbands, women with workaholic husbands, women with truck-driver husbands,
and women with evangelist husbands may all find
themselves the sole parent their children can depend
on for day-to-day care. This is a vast number of women,
and we haven't even considered those mothers with
sinful or rebellious husbands or those women who
took the reins of leadership from their well-intentioned
husband when the children were small, and then, to
their dismay, found it impossible to reverse that decision when they were twelve.

The good news is that these situations are far from
hopeless. Yes, parenting was designed by God to take
two. Yes, it is far more difficult to do the job alone. Yes,
it is confusing, frustrating, and exhausting. But it can
be done. God is still on the throne, and the prayer and
faith of a godly mother have turned more than a few
children toward the Lord even when the odds seemed
impossible.

This chapter is not designed to be a full treatment on
child rearing. I would refer the reader to the many
other excellent works available on that subject from
your local Christian bookstore. I would also encourage

mothers to know that while two-parent families are the norm and most books talk about the need for a father to take certain roles, most good advice given to two parents can be incorporated by one parent if it is only one parent who is willing to read the book! My purpose for this chapter is to give specific hope to mothers who are left to do the job alone. We'll approach a few of their particular struggles and fears.

One of the fears I hear women express is the fear of homosexuality. When a woman is left to raise boys, she has fewer guidelines than with girls. After all, she has never been a boy. Her son's sexual development and gender identity can be very intimidating problems to the mother.

I can sympathize with her. I have no problem at all discussing sexual issues with men or boys in my office, but I remember being very tongue-tied as I struggled with my own sons. Often the mother will have deep concerns about the possibility of producing a homosexual son who identifies so much with her that he forgets how to be a man.

Mothers frequently have no idea of what is normal or abnormal sexual behavior, and these may not be the type of questions she is comfortable discussing with her dad or brother or even family doctor. If her son is three years old and enjoys playing dolls with his sister, should she worry? Will not having a father around hurt his male development? Is a bad father better than no father? Is it natural for a five-year-old to have an erection? Is he thinking about sexual things?

WHAT ABOUT HOMOSEXUALITY AND MY SON?
Homosexuality can happen in any family. There are no absolute guarantees for even the Christian home, but

the closest thing to a deterrent as shown by recent research is a father/son relationship that is marked by warm affection and mutual respect. A relationship such as this seems to make a boy comfortable and secure about who he is as a male, and thus cross-sexual relationships can be developed without fear. There also seems to be some indication that a mother who is overprotective or domineering toward her son will encourage homosexual tendencies.

That leaves many women between a rock and a hard place. Maybe she would love to see her son have a warm and respectful relationship with his dad, but what if dad won't or can't or isn't around to provide that? When she is shell-shocked by a life that has kicked her in the teeth, it is a natural reaction to be overprotective. And if she is the only parent or the only one with any guts, how can she *not* dominate the family?

The answers to the puzzling questions of how we can raise reasonable children in an unreasonable situation will always be found in the mother's faith. When there is no father who can be respected, when a woman's fear is causing her to be overprotective of her children, or when her anger is driving her to dominate and control, faith is the solution.

To some that may sound too "religious" to be practical, but from both experience and the Word of God, I know that it is workable and real. Faith is the answer. Let's take all three of the things that encourage homosexual behavior—lack of respect for the father, overprotection by the mother, and domination by the mother—and see how these are cured by real faith.

Notice that I said *real* faith. Not simply going to church. Not prayers that are little more than desperation thrown on the air. Not a salvation experience we had as a child that has had little impact on our life since that time. These are not evidence of real faith.

Real faith believes something. It looks at circumstances, yet leans on things that cannot be seen. It depends on, bets on, relies on the reality of a living, personal God who is actively involved in life.

That kind of faith can be an active agent in our struggle to respect our child's father. Faith lets us believe that God has a purpose for everything and everyone. If flies and snakes have their place in God's ecology and serve His purpose in the end, surely one stubborn man can fit into His plan as well. Our belief that the father of our child has worth and purpose in God's sight helps him gain worth in our sight also. By faith we can gain the strength to look past what a man does and respect him as a unique creation of God.

If our husband has hurt us, our belief that God takes all things and works them together for our eventual benefit will make a real difference.As our attitude changes, our son's attitude can be changed as well. By our example a boy can learn to see life honestly and still respect both his dad and himself.

Faith will also be crucial for a woman troubled by fear and/or loneliness who has a tendency to become overprotective toward her sons.

I remember when my own boys were small and we had moved to the ranch. One spring afternoon I stood by the back screen door watching them disappear out of sight down the path to the shallow creek. At that time they must have been around ages ten and eight. They had spent a lot of time in the pastures with Bill or me while work was being done, but this time they would be out of my field of vision and alone. It was almost more than I could bear.

I had thought about this decision for weeks. I wanted the boys to be free to roam the home place and experience life in the country, but part of me was so frightened that breathing actually hurt. What would happen to them out there? What if one of them broke a leg or was bitten by a poisonous snake? What if they came across a squirrel that had rabies or a pack of wild dogs or if they ran into one of the few wolves that were still in the county? I could see all kinds of horror pictures rising in my mind.

I knew all of those things were highly unlikely, but they were possible, and I was afraid. Only as I believed in a real God who saw those boys when I could not did I have strength to let them go. Faith in God's ability to care for them helped keep me from holding them so tightly that they became as fearful as I was. Faith gave my boys wonderful memories of swinging on grapevines and picking fresh berries in the spring instead of being confined to the yard.

I realize that my situation of country living was unusual, and I want to be very clear that there is a line between trusting God and failing to carry out the responsibility God gave us to care for and watch our children. God is not a glorified baby-sitter, but He is a secure tower of protection and strength when we need Him. Faith in God's care of our children can keep a woman from becoming fearful and overprotective.

Faith is also the determining factor in softening a dominating mother.

Sometimes it is hard for a person to determine if she is dominating or simply doing a job. In her book, *Mothers and Sons*, Jean Lush provides a good contrast between a mother who dominates and a mother who is simply forced to lead and be responsible.

A dominating mother talks all the time and does not listen to what her children try to tell her. She chops off their comments before they are finished and rushes into giving answers and directions before all the facts are collected. She tells others what to do, gives advice before others ask for it, and acts as if she knows more than others around her. In most cases she is very organized and efficient in performing tasks, but she railroads people in the process.

A mother who leads her children takes time to listen to their thoughts and feelings. She doesn't pretend to have all the answers, and she avoids jumping to conclusions. When her children ask for help, she is willing to assist them, but her goal is to help them learn, not to do everything for them.[*]

Both men and women can fall into the trap of trying to dominate everything about them. Sometimes they are simply following the examples of their own parents, sometimes pride has led them to a sense of entitlement, and sometimes they dominate as an overreaction to the fear of being out of control. But whatever the cause, the solution is faith.

A faith that believes God is in ultimate control, that He is well able and willing to take ultimate responsibility, and that it is safe to trust Him will produce a believer who is able to relax. She will be able to let go of fear. The sense of entitlement will be eliminated as she realizes the ground is level at the foot of the cross: She stands no higher than anyone else and no lower. This faith will even let her know the fatherhood of God well enough to give her a new example to follow. She will

---

[*]Jean Lush, *Mothers and Sons* (Old Tappan, New Jersey: Revell, 1988), 106.

not be chained to repeat the mistakes of her parents.

There are no guarantees against homosexuality. But a mother who uses her faith to build the best relationship possible between her son and his father and by faith achieves a balance between being an overprotective mom and a dominating one will have eliminated the three main family patterns that appear to encourage homosexual development in boys. By the way, she will have also eliminated the three main family patterns that create disturbed girls as well!

ARE YOU MY CHILD, MY SPOUSE, OR MY FRIEND?

Another trap that is easy for a woman to fall into when she is raising children alone is that of letting the children slowly become substitutes for healthy adult relationships. Her seven-year-old son becomes the one she turns to when she wants a sympathetic ear to listen to financial problems. Her twelve-year-old daughter becomes her best friend with whom she shares everything from makeup to dating secrets. These children are forced to take adult roles far too soon, and the emotional damage may not show up for years. Children can emotionally take the place of adult friends or even the place of the spouse.

I recall one client who was well into her thirties before the strain of constantly being her mother's only friend, confidante, advisor, and source of happiness brought her close to a breakdown. She could remember when she was only seven the long conversations she and Mom would have as mother poured out her heart about her marriage troubles. In this case, by age twelve the little girl was even made a confidante when Mom decided she would help along Daddy's heart condition by feeding him fatty, high-cholesterol foods in the hope that he would have a heart attack and die.

When children take on the roles of adults and adults begin to lean on children for support, we call it an "upside down" family. The results are devastating. Not many families are so extreme that the children are made conspirators in Daddy's death, but the demand that children grow up too fast and provide for the parents' needs instead of vice versa is all too common.

However, I can sympathize with mothers who fall into this pattern. I have been a single parent, and I remember the deep, internal pain. It was a shock when *everything* suddenly started being my job. There was no release. Week after week, day after day, all the decisions, all the discipline, all the responsibility, was constantly mine.

At times I felt it would crush me. I longed for someone—anyone!—who would shoulder the burden with me. It would have been oh, so easy, to let Wesley make the decisions and do the work of running the ranch, to let Billy carry all my anger and frustration, to snuggle up to Nancy at night when I was lonely, and to make Lori stay home and take over as mother to the other children. In fact, this was so tempting and such a well-recognized danger that I nearly erred on the other side. I worked so hard at letting Lori live her own life that I nearly convinced her I had no need of her.

The balancing act between building warm, trusting relationships with our children and treating them like adults long before they are ready is a delicate one. It should have a big label pasted across it reading Caution, Handle with Prayer! This problem is complicated even more because of the need for all hands to pitch in and help when one spouse will not or cannot do his job.

Another complication: the natural tendency of some children to take on an adult role even when not asked.

One woman who was a young child when her dad died clearly remembers that when she and Mom went walking downtown after that, she took care to always walk on the outside of the sidewalk. The old-fashioned custom of a gentleman taking his wife's arm and walking between her and the traffic was a part of what this little girl saw as a father's protective role. Mom had no one to protect her, so the little girl took his place.

The mom never noticed this subtle shift, but inside the child was feeling the need to take Dad's place and protect Mom. In reality, the little girl could carry almost no real responsibility, but emotionally she thought of herself as Mom's protector and carried the burden just as though it were real. She felt responsible to analyze, understand, and fix all situations and control threats. Of course, her task was impossible and frustrating.

As an adult, this woman was still a controller who was determined to fix all threats by understanding and analyzing all things and governing the ungovernable. Her efforts at control and frustration over a life and a family that refused to be controlled led to depression. The beginnings of this problem were when as a little girl she tried to take on the responsibility of a missing dad.

It is good for children to take on some responsibilities, but these must be age-appropriate and tempered with an understanding that the adult is still the adult. It might be altogether proper to confide your desire for a job change with a son who is twenty-five and in graduate school or a married daughter of twenty-one, but it is altogether improper to discuss those details with a ten-year-old no matter how mature he is or how willing to listen.

Children can also provide comfort and some social interaction for a woman who raises them alone, but they should never be so much a part of Mom's world that they have no room to develop worlds of their own. Raised with the freedom to become adults themselves, children can turn out to be our best friends, but they must become adults first. That can sound like a lot of lonely years while we wait for them to grow, but the wait will be worth it. I cannot think of a greater reward than to have our children grow up and one day call their mom "blessed" (Proverbs 31:28). To me, that sounds like the best friendship of all.

THE AMAZING INFLUENCE OF A MAN

There were many frustrating things about being a single mom. One that really ticked me off was the way I could say something five hundred times and the kids never heard me, but a man could say something once and it was immediately accepted as gospel. When the girls were old enough to date, it was the boyfriend who had clear insight to all truth while Mom's ideas were subject to question. For the boys it seemed that a man—any man—was bound to have more sense than poor, struggling Mom. It might have been something their dad said years before about how a ranch should be run or something a schoolteacher, a friend's dad, or a man from church said. But as long as the words came from someone who wore britches, it was bound to be good advice. This was most pointedly brought home to me in one of my many rounds with Billy.

Because I was a widow and needed a driver to help me run the ranch and get the children to school, I was able to get Billy a hardship driver's license when he was only fourteen (Texas law has changed since then). Both boys had been driving tractors and trucks in the fields since before they could reach the foot controls, so skill was not a problem, but cooperation definitely was.

It was Billy's job to pick up his brother and sister after school and bring them home to the ranch about ten miles out of town. On one particular Friday, Billy needed his band uniform from the cleaners to perform at the football game that night, but he had forgotten to get money from me that morning. In our small town the lack of money was not really a big problem because he could tell the lady behind the counter that he would come by the next day, and she would probably give him the uniform without question. But having his brother and sister see him in this compromising position was to be avoided at all cost. Billy pulled up at the cleaners and, with his most commanding voice, told them to stay in the truck. Of course, they immediately got out and followed him into the store. The argument that followed was intense, and it continued as they headed down the highway for home.

To this day I am not exactly sure who said what, but in the end Billy pulled the truck over to the side of the road, and Wesley got out and slammed the door. Billy drove on down the road a short way and pulled over again. He knew he couldn't come home without his brother because I would kill him. His pride would not let him go back to get Wesley, and Wesley was not about to sacrifice his own pride by walking the few hundred feet to the truck, so they both stubbornly sat. Nancy finally got tired of the standoff and started walking up and down the road between the brothers trying to make some kind of compromise so everyone could get home before dark. Never underestimate the negotiating power of a nine-year-old because somehow all the kids and the truck were home before I got in from the pasture.

Any mother can imagine what kind of buzz saw I ran into the moment I stepped through the door. Billy was yelling in one ear about how Wesley had caused trouble, and Wesley was defending himself loudly in my other ear saying it was all to be blamed on Billy's stubbornness. Nancy was in front of me trying to interpret each boy's wrath and get credit for getting everyone home. I pulled off my leather gloves and cowboy hat and threw them on the kitchen bar and listened. And listened. And hung my head with weariness and listened some more. If Solomon had been standing in that kitchen with all of his wisdom, he could never have come to a solution that all three kids would have thought fair.

My judgment was that each boy was wrong, and each had been punished enough, but in an effort to satisfy the wrath that was still steaming from each male body, I gave a mild—very mild—punishment to each and told them to forget the matter.

Wesley grumbled and sputtered like a piece of broken machinery grinding to a halt, but Billy would not let the matter drop. He argued for hours. He wouldn't even shut up when I refused to talk back to him. He just stood his ground and kept his half of the gripe going strong. When suppertime came, he refused to eat with a family that was so stubborn they couldn't see things his way.

He openly admitted that it was not the punishment he minded; it was the principle of the thing! I reminded him that he did not have to believe I was right, he just had to obey. He could believe I was wrong and say so, but he could not force me to agree with him. He did not have to agree with me or tell me I was right or think it was fair. All he had to do was obey because that was what the Bible said a son should do for his mother. The Bible did not tell him that he had to feel a certain way or that we must agree.

Billy insisted that I was wrong, and he was furious. He was determined that I must change my mind and declare him totally innocent. We had been in to see the pastor for counseling a couple of times before, so Billy demanded that I make an appointment with the preacher so he could tell me I was wrong. Unfortunately, the preacher was out of town on a deer hunt and would not be back for four days. It was a long four days.

Brother Andy burst into laughter when he heard our story. "Billy," he said with a grin, "you don't have to agree with your mother or think she is fair, all you have to do is obey." Billy looked at him with a pleasant but serious expression and said, "Oh, now I understand." I almost fell through the bottom of the chair. I had been living for days with an unreasonable, yammering ball of fury who never heard a word I said, but as soon as the same words came out of a man's mouth he suddenly "understood." I would have jumped on the middle of his chest with both feet and beat on his head . . . but I was just too tired!

I did learn one thing, however. As long as my kids were going to value the advice of a man and be influenced by the men around them, I needed to help create situations where a man's influence would be good.

At first I thought along the lines of one man for each kid. A patient, wise male, someone who would offer to take my boys on weekend camping trips. A wise teacher-type who could give my girls an example of godly manhood and respect.

But it quickly became obvious that my ideas of what

should be were unworkable. Like the old song says, "A good man nowadays is hard to find"! Rather than seeing the solution as one man, I needed to see many men playing small parts in each of my children's lives.

I suspect that every mom will have to find her own men in her own places, but these are some of the places I found mine. Unlike most widows, I had more money after Bill died than we had while he was alive, and I enrolled my kids in a private Christian school. I wanted them to have the educational advantages that I felt a school like this might offer, but far more important than academics was the fact that the principal was a man who I knew took a keen, personal interest in each student at this small school. It also had a couple of male teachers, and a pastor or two were floating around much of the time.

I also took advantage of opportunities to invite visiting pastors or evangelical teams to the house. Any time the church asked for volunteers to feed or house a pastor, my hand was the first one up. I also hosted youth and children's parties and consistently asked families to join us for dinner after church. Usually I would issue these invitations for two or more families at a time so that the men would feel more comfortable than they might having dinner with a single woman and her children only.

When my brother showed an interest in Billy, I quickly made arrangements for Billy to stay with him for a week during the summer even though he lived downstate. It was not just so I could get Billy out of my hair but so Billy could be under his influence. When a man at church was kind to one of my children, I went out of my way to mention how much I appreciated his thoughtfulness. Even though it hurt my ego, I used my pastor as a family counselor.

And, last of all, I spent many hours on the road taking the boys to the homes of other boys and dads who I thought might be a good male example.

I don't know where you will find your men. Organized sports, church youth groups, band, scouting programs—all provide the opportunity for children to be influenced by men. Check out the men who run these things. Don't send your kids off to them blindly. Are they the kind of men you want shaping your children? If they are—or even if they are acceptable though maybe not all you had hoped for—encourage your kids to join.

A word of caution may be needed here. We must depend heavily on the Spirit of God to guide us in the decisions of whom to trust with our children. Horror stories about sex abuse exist even in long-honored civic groups and the church. We dare not let this fear paralyze us, but we do need to be wise and deal with reality. Just remember that God is faithful, and He will help us guard our children well.

Do you have a godly brother or father or uncle who might be willing to let the boys spend a week with them during the summer? Is there a local church that has team teaching in the Sunday school so that your little girl's class will have both a male and a female teacher? You might need to change churches or move to get the kind of influence you want and they need, but even those measures are possible for a determined woman.

Male counselors are also a good source of influence. If you can find one who is a Christian or a support group for teens run by a Christian man, you are very blessed. You may have to look hard because these are rare birds, but if you can find a good one, it is well worth the effort.

Pray about the male influence in your child's life. Be

on guard agains... ...nce. Ask
God to show y... ...need.
Pray. Pray. P... ...
answers, ...
influen... ...
shak... ...
tha... ...n
... ...
...hears-
b... ...on the
Bill! ... ...y, "Hey,
... g this bass
part!" It ... climbed the
steps and to... remember
glancing behin... at his tennis shoes
barely touched the ... up tall and shared a
book with Brother Lon... choir was informal
and no one came unglued ...en a boy well below the
accepted age of membership slowly became a part of
the team. At that time, Billy's father never came to
church, and my heart was overflowing with gratitude at
the kindness of Christian friends who made room for
one lonely little boy and a man who took time to invite
him to "join us men."

The influence of a godly father who builds warm,
respectful relationships with his sons and daughters
cannot be overestimated. It is ideal to have a man like
that lead his family. But if a woman finds herself alone
to do the job, this does not mean the situation is hopeless or even that it can never be good. The good news is
that God's arm is not so short that He cannot reach into
even the darkest situation and pull out a sane mother
and well-adjusted children. God asked Israel why they
did not turn to Him when the going got tough: "Was
my arm too short to ransom you? Do I lack the strength

to rescue you?" And He might well ask us the same questions one day when we stand before Him.

Women can raise children to be well-adjusted, stable adults. No, it isn't easy. In fact, it is downright hard. But it is never impossible, for when God is put in the equation, nothing shall ever be impossible (Luke 1:37).

TEN

I HATE TO GO

ABOVE YOU

At the beginning of this book, I told how it felt to stand outside in the snow and look through a window at a warm, Christian family inside. I told of the cold pain and how much I wanted my home to be like the one inside the house. I had felt cheated because my husband did not provide what I thought he should.

For the last nine chapters, I have shared with you the steps I took to come in out of the snow. I am convinced that no woman needs to stand in the snow forever. We can move into that lovely, warm room by using the keys God has already given us and by understanding that our expectations of what a Christian home is may be different from what the Bible shows it to be.

I knew I had made it inside because of the things I felt within and the changes I saw in my attitude. I stopped feeling bitter and cheated. I accepted the fact that God wanted me to bloom where I was planted, not spend my time in grief over where I was not. Bill was still in rebellion against the Lord he had once served, our financial problems were horrendous, leadership was far from the Pauline model, alcohol and some drugs became a part of family reality toward the last, and we never lived in a Victorian home.

But even though outside circumstances never changed, the me inside did change, and that made a real difference. There was pain, but it was mixed with rest. There was fear, but it was always mixed with hope. There was loneliness, but it was always mixed with comfort.

Above all, I learned to love—really love—Bill because I respected him and accepted the fact that the Trinity was not a quartet; God the Father, the Holy Spirit, and Jesus had things well in hand. I was free to sit in a chair and knit and leave the driving to Them.

My journey from the snow to the warm fireside wasn't quick or easy, and I doubt that yours will be. Before I leave you to travel on your own, I will add one last chapter to explore a couple of the strange things that you may find once inside the room. One of the strangest is that the room is not a place where all your needs are met immediately and all pain is totally gone.

LESSONS FROM EDEN

Back in chapter 1, I made a promise to the reader that I would finish discussing what God said to Eve when Paradise slipped away and her world was drastically changed. In that chapter we examined in detail what I believe God meant when He told her that her desire would from that moment on draw her to her husband. In chapter 2 we discussed what it meant to have a husband "rule" over her and why God chose men to be leaders. Now we need to see the last statement God made to Eve. This last statement not only has affected our lives while we stood in the snow, but also it will impact us after we have moved into the warmth of a true Christian home, and we need to be prepared to face and understand that impact.

When the world fell apart, God made specific statements to the snake, to Adam, and to Eve. He cursed the snake. He cursed the ground. But when it came to humans, the term *curse* is not used. God simply told them what the world they had chosen would be like and how it would be different from Paradise. God said to the woman:

> I will greatly increase your pains in childbearing;
> with pain you will give birth to children.
> Your desire will be for your husband,
> and he will rule over you. (Genesis 3:16, NIV)

Have you ever wondered why God did that? Why mix pain with childbirth? Why not, perhaps, put her nose on upside down or make her bald? Why did God take one of the most fulfilling times in a woman's life and mix it with trouble? To find our answer, let's backtrack a little.

We will start by taking a look at the two special trees God planted in His garden and the mystery of their names. God named these trees. He called them *The Tree of Life* and *The Tree of the Knowledge of Good and Evil*. The Bible tells us that the Tree of Life would do exactly what its name implied. It would give eternal, physical life. God knew eternal, earthly life was not good for man in his sinful condition, so He blocked man's access to this tree (Genesis 3:22-24). But man had already eaten from the Tree of the Knowledge of Good and Evil, and the fruit of that tree was already working in his life.

We often think of the word *evil* as a synonym for *sin*, but that is not necessarily the case. Evil can be a much broader word that covers everything that is hurtful or bad or worthless or to be rejected (see Jeremiah 24). It is the same for the word *good*. It can be used to describe something that is sinless; however, it is most often used to include beauty and joy and hope and all those things we would want as part of our lives forever. I believe it is in this broader definition that the Tree of the Knowledge of Good and Evil got its name.

The word *knowledge* implies a personal and experiential kind of knowing. Something like when Adam "knew" his wife and she conceived a child.

Eve wanted to know good and evil. She wanted to experience them both, hold them both, be able to examine them "up close and personal," and rightly judge the value of each. This was the prize knowledge that she thought would make her wise and like God. When she took the fruit, she reached for a life that would be woven of a mixture of everything that could be rightly called good (joyful, pretty, productive, hopeful, etc.) and everything that could rightly be called bad (sad, ugly, empty, useless, etc.). Eve got what she asked for. So did Adam. So did we, their children.

All human history since that point has been one long struggle as individuals and nations learn about good and evil. The tension between these two extremes is the core of every movie plot, every novel, every political stance, every philosophy, every religion, every war, every human life. The struggle will continue until at last a new heaven and a new earth are formed, and good and evil are for all eternity completely and totally separate. Everything that is evil will eventually take its place in the Lake of Fire, and all good will gather in the presence of God. Until that future time comes, the struggle between good and evil will continue to be part of human experience.

When God chose to mix pain with childbirth, He gave Eve a searing example that she could not avoid in her very flesh. In those few hours of childbirth, a woman goes through some of the most intense suffering and some of the greatest rejoicing that can be experienced in life. She also takes part in the unfathomable question of how good and evil relate to each other and to us humans. Does pain become a good thing when it produces something good? I have known barren women who would regard transition labor as a good thing because it would be the path to achieving their heart's desire. How can we reject the pain of life without sealing ourselves off from the enjoyment of the wonderful?

Good and evil are so intricately entwined that total separation and understanding are impossible to our finite minds. What we think is evil at one point in time proves to be the path to rejoicing at another.

By the way, this same mix of good and evil was to be in Adam's life in a specific way also. For him, God mixed pain with work. Ecclesiastes 3:13 states that a man should find satisfaction in his work and that work is a gift from God. However, Ecclesiastes 1:3-9 says that there is nothing to be gained from work because it is all to be done over and over again with no permanent progress ever made. So is work good or evil? It is both. It is a mixture. For a man (or woman) to work day after day to survive, pay bills, grow old, and die is the ultimate vanity. But it is also true that working and being able to provide for themselves and their families is, for most men, a source of satisfaction and identity.

The snake told Eve that this intimate knowledge of good and evil would make her like God. He was not lying. That is exactly what happened. As the Trinity discussed the Fall among themselves, God said, "The man has now become like one of us, knowing good and evil"

(Genesis 3:22, NIV). I will leave to wiser minds than mine to figure out all that is implied with that statement, but I will note one way that God is impacted by evil. Using the broad definition for evil that I gave earlier, God experienced the bad, ugly, painful side of life in Christ. When the Word became flesh and dwelt among us (John 1:14), absolute goodness experienced absolute evil as Jesus was made sin for us (2 Corinthians 5:21).

The impact that the Fall had on all people cannot be overestimated. The strange world that began at that moment is still the world we live in today. For women, we still experience the drawing that calls our desire toward husband and home. We also live in a world where men rule over us. And we experience pain in childbirth. All of Eve's burdens were given us, her daughters, as well. And life becomes a daily experience of both good and evil in a tangled knot.

We will never untangle this knot until heaven. Getting out of the snow and realizing that we *are* a Christian family right where we live will not free us from this daily experience. But then, having Prince Charming for a husband and/or a godly leader at the front of our home would not unravel the tangle either. It is beyond the power of a woman to free herself, and it is beyond the power of a good husband to do it for her. The only solution is to grow in Christ enough to rest even in the middle of the mess. Our freedom is internal and spirit-based, not external and husband-based.

One of the most consistent phenomena that I see in my office is the surprise and insult that many people feel because life is not "right." Somehow we expected it to be so different. It seems to me that women in particular have walked out of Eden with a built-in echo of a memory of Paradise. We want life now to fit what life must have been like then. And too often we are tricked into believing that if our man would only behave as he should and be the leader he should that Eden in this life would be restored. We are wrong.

When the Apostle Peter was old, he wrote a letter to younger Christians. It was addressed to those who were strangers in the world (1 Peter 1:1, NIV)—people who felt out of place and slightly disjointed from the flow of life. The whole letter is about troubles and what they mean for the believer.

Peter talked about suffering when all you ever wanted to do was to live right and what it is like to be punished unjustly. He talked about submission to people who are cruel and how different we Christians are from the rest of humanity. He talked specifically of wives who are married to unbelieving husbands. Peter said a lot of precious things in this book, but I believe the verse that has meant the most to me is verse 12 of chapter 4: "Dear friends, do not be surprised at the painful trial you are suffering, as though something strange were happening to you" (1 Peter 4:12, NIV).

When we accept the fact that we are strangers in a world that is fallen and broken and decaying, we will have taken our first step toward real peace.

It may seem strange or even unfair that no matter how much your husband improves, life will not be Eden. It is a trap of the devil to draw a woman's heart to a misty perfection of someday. He too often entices her to believe that life would be fixed if her man would only get fixed. This creates a breeding ground for resentment and bitter disappointment when the ideal is never reached no matter how much she tries to pound her husband into shape.

Oh, I agree that life would certainly be easier if all men were the kind of men God said they should be. But then, life would be easier if all women were what God said they should be, too.

Don't be discouraged when life or your man or your heart is not what it should be. God is not finished with His project yet. Know that even when you move from the snow to the warm home, there will be struggles—real and painful struggles. The difference will be what takes place inside yourself. Peace, contentment, strength, and wisdom will grow instead of bitterness and despair.

I want you to avoid the devil's trap of unrealistic expectations, but there are two more traps that I would like to briefly mention. These traps are set just inside the door, and they can catch you before you are three steps from the snow. Some women get caught and return to the snow, thinking ice is more pleasant than traps. The first trap is guilt we feel inside because we are becoming more holy than our husbands, and the second is condemnation that can come from the outside because we are changing.

THE GUILT TRAP

As I grew as a Christian, I experienced guilt over being more holy than my husband. I no longer staggered under the oppressive weight of submission to a man. Now I was sure of myself as a servant in submission to the King of kings, and the service I gave my husband and my family was an outworking of my service to the King. It was as if I had switched masters. Bill was not my master; Jesus was. I was submissive to Bill only because I was following the instruction of my Lord.

This new way of living felt good. But I also felt guilty about feeling good. I was puzzled. How could I serve the Lord, feel good about myself, recognize and rejoice

over the freedom and growth Jesus was giving me, and
not feel pride? Had I put myself "above" Bill?

For myself, this floating guilt over possible sinful
pride was a real problem. Every time I felt myself getting up off the floor, guilt would come along and condemn me for feeling good. I thought this was the Holy
Spirit trying to keep me humble, but in time I saw it
was only echoes of lies I had believed since childhood.

Each child has its own filter through which it inter-
prets life. I don't blame my parents or my church for
the way I interpreted their teaching on humility, but
somehow I picked up that if I tried real hard and won a
prize, I should never feel special; only God should get
glory. If I got a new dress, it was wrong to feel pretty
because many other little girls didn't have such clothes.
If anyone gave me a compliment, the proper response
was, "Oh, no, I really didn't do very well, but thanks anyway." It was all right to send someone a picture of your
dog, but vanity to send someone a picture of yourself!
Needless to say, the echoes of this philosophy made it
very difficult for me to enjoy the fruit that God was producing in my life.

THE THREAT TRAP

Added to our problematic personal reactions to the
growth we see in our lives is the reaction that such
growth causes when others see it.

If a woman is married to a nonbeliever or to a Christian who is in rebellion, her spiritual progress can be a
threat to her husband. She doesn't have to do or say
anything for him to feel condemned. Walking into the
bedroom and catching her in prayer, listening to her
read a Bible story to the kids, lying in bed while she
dresses the kids and leaves for church are all enough to

make a man's conscience smart. This process becomes more intense when the Holy Spirit begins to tromp all over him!

When a man is feeling one peg down as he measures himself against his wife's holiness, guess what he is likely to do. Of course! He will put out every effort to convince her that *she* is as sinful as *he* feels! One thing he is likely to accuse her of is pride.

I have never suffered this problem myself, but many of my clients have, and their husbands throw some very piercing knives as they try to drag their wives down to their own level. I have heard them use such daggers as: "If you were really half as good as you think you are . . ." "Who do you think you are trying to fool with that Christian garbage?" "What is little Miss Goody-Two-Shoes doing now?" "What are you really after down there at that church? What is his name?"

It can be a desperate struggle to hold to a godly kind of rejoicing that gives birth to good self-esteem when we are under attack from our own misguided conscience and/or the condemnation of others.

GROWING AND LOVING

As I mentioned, for myself the attack came more from within than from without, but the struggle was very real. How could I be humble and still know I was spiritually more mature than my husband, who was supposed to be my leader? I found part of my solution to this strange problem in a strange place.

One day while going through a large, old volume of poetry that I found on a bottom shelf in my pastor's study, I discovered a special poem. It was not a religious poem at all, but it spoke directly to my problem and settled it. I have looked for this poem many times since then, but I have never been able to find it or remember the author. However, I do remember the story it told.

In the poem, a man has returned to the little one-room school where he grew up. The school has been abandoned for many years and the peeling paint, a broken window, and an empty swing moving in the wind give the place a feeling of loneliness. The sun has just begun to set and shadows are growing longer as the man begins to remember a crisp fall day from his childhood when he stood on the porch of the old school with a little girl. School had been dismissed for several minutes, and most of the other kids had run down the dusty roads anxious to get home. But he and the little girl stood for a moment, each intensely aware of the other, but both afraid to speak.

The girl twisted the corner of her gingham apron with small pale hands and looked at her shoes. In a moment she spoke and began to apologize. She told him that she really didn't mean to spell the word right and beat him in the contest. Then she looked up with tearful, blue eyes and said, "I hate to go above you because, you see, I love you."

The grown man sighs deeply as he remembers. He marvels at the tenderness, sensitivity, and humility of the girl. He has traveled on for many years in the dog-eat-dog competitiveness of modern life and he knows how rare—how very rare—it is for someone to get the best of him at life and then feel a twinge of pain because they love him and regret going above him.

There is a regret and a twinge of pain involved in going above anyone we truly love. It is not pride. It is not passing judgment on another. It is only recognizing that by God's written standard, the way we have chosen is better than the choices of our mate.

Some might conclude that it is best to stop the progress. Maybe we should avoid future spiritual growth, or even go backward. If we love our mate, we don't want to leave him behind—not intellectually, not socially, not emotionally, not financially, and most certainly not spiritually. Yet when we examine the true fruits of spirituality, we see that going above someone is not a negative thing, but a positive.

If our spiritual growth is real (Galatians 5:22-23), it will increase our love for our mate. It will create in us a joy and a peace and a patience that endure when times are tough. We will be more kind and seek to do good things for our mate, improve our relationship, and be continually faithful. Our attitude will be one of gentleness. And when tough decisions have to be made or tempers begin to rise, our self-control will keep us from saying or doing things we might later regret. Personal spiritual growth may create a feeling of separateness in a marriage if only one of the partners seeks the Lord. But if a marriage fails, it cannot be blamed on the spiritual growth of one partner. That would be like blaming a marriage breakup on the fact that one partner had too much honest, open love and faithfulness.

I cannot think of a worse marriage scenario than for two people to be striving to outdo and go above each other intellectually, socially, emotionally, or financially. But I can think of no stronger marriage than for two people to be committed to outracing each other in spiritual growth and love.

As we move out of the snow and determine to use our keys to make our home a Christian home, the keys will be used mostly on our own heart and our own obedience to our Lord. We can say to our mate with an honest and humble heart, "I have decided to go above you because I want to honestly love you."